© 2022 Experiments in Fiction and Gabriela Marie Milton.
https://experimentsinfiction.com

Gabriela Marie Milton
Wounds I Healed: The Poetry of Strong Women

Published by: Experiments in Fiction

Text Design by: Experiments in Fiction

Cover Design by: Experiments in Fiction

Cover Art by: Nick Reeves © 2022

ISBN-10: 1 73975 772 4

ISBN-13: 978 1 73975 772 4

WOUNDS I HEALED:

THE POETRY OF STRONG WOMEN

**A SPACE WHERE WOMEN AND MEN'S VOICES COME TOGETHER
TO TESTIFY TO THE CHALLENGES WOMEN FACE IN OUR
SOCIETY AND TO THEIR POWER TO OVERCOME THEM**

Edited and curated by Gabriela Marie Milton
Published by Experiments in Fiction, 2022

Wounds I Healed:

The Poetry of Strong Women

GABRIELA MARIE MILTON (ED.)

"I am too intelligent, too demanding, and too resourceful for anyone to be able to take charge of me entirely."

— Simone de Beauvoir

"In the midst of winter, I found there was, within me, an invincible summer.

And that makes me happy. For it says that no matter how hard the world pushes against me, within me, there's something stronger - something better, pushing right back."

— Albert Camus

GABRIELA MARIE MILTON (ED.)

Editor's Note on the Book

When I posted the call for submissions to *Wounds I Healed: The Poetry of Strong Women*, I wanted to compile an anthology that would underscore how powerful women are, and how much they can accomplish regardless of the adversities most of them go through. I had no idea that – while reading the poems I included in this book – a larger story would emerge. I can only judge this story with my own sensibility.

First, there is my complicity with the poems from the book. I am a woman, and I can relate to the consequences that our patriarchal society has on my fellow women. The stories the poems here tell are my stories even if I did not live them all. Either Jung's "objective psyche" exists, or I underwent a process of osmosis while reading the stunning work I selected. All abuses described here, as well as all victories, became mine.

Second, I can assure you dear readers that you will not regret a moment immersing yourselves in this book. It is not important whether a poem is born like a child, or constructed like a temple. The type of poetry is always secondary to its substance. It's a matter of preference. The poems in this book are poems of substance regardless of their form. They grab you by the throat. They scream listen to me. They bring you to your knees. They inscribe on each page - with a multiplicity of voices coming from all sexes – the astonishing power women have. They are exceptional poems.

Third, is this a feminist book? One could see it as such regardless of what definition of feminism one employs. However, our minds and souls can transcend definitions. We can go beyond reflections. The poems in this book are not reflections or merely copies of life. They do not belong to certain metaphysics of feminism and/or patriarchy. The poems in this book are life itself.

Welcome to women's lives my dear readers.

Enjoy the ride.

Gabriela Marie Milton
Editor

#1 Amazon Bestselling Author of :

Woman: Splendor and Sorrow: Love Poems and Poetic Prose
(Vita Brevis Press, 2021)

Passions: Love Poems and Other Writings
(Vita Brevis Press, 2020)

Publisher's Note on the Book

I have just finished reading through the manuscript of *Wounds I Healed* for a second time, and I cannot overstate what an important collection of poems this volume represents. To read these poems is to undertake an emotional journey: through the dark depths of physical and psychological abuse, via the perils of chronic illness and the pains of pregnancy loss, crossing all manner of nightmare landscapes to emerge into the serene pastures of healing and recovery.

What a journey our lives as women represent! I write this as a woman myself, but have the utmost respect for the male contributors to this anthology who have been sensitive enough to observe women's experience and applaud their strength and fortitude in weathering so many storms.

To truly heal a wound, we must first acknowledge its presence. We must then look at the cause of the wound, and what steps we must take in order to repair it. Such healing work can represent the endeavour of a lifetime, but what magnificent poetry sings in the wake of such endeavour! I leave you to this volume, and let the Poetry of Strong Women speak for itself....

Ingrid Wilson
Publisher, Experiments In Fiction

Previous publications:

The Anthropocene Hymnal (July 2021)

40 Poems At 40 (February 2022)

Contents

15

POEMS

GABRIELA MARIE MILTON (ED.)

Claudette Colvin, Rosa Parks, We Thank You Both Equally
by Mark Andrew Heathcote

Refusing to give up her seat to a white woman
soon to become a civil rights activist, Claudette Colvin
was first arrested at the tender age of 15.
in Montgomery, Alabama, for simply sitting
on a crowded, segregated bus Claudette Colvin
she crossed swords with the state on a-number-of-issues.
It leaves me blue with a dry mouth
that there ever was a Montgomery bus boycott.

It makes my guts twist and knot thinking how it took
the United States Supreme Court to make a decision
to declare segregated buses were unconstitutional
civil rights activist Claudette Colvin
was first arrested at the tender age of 15.
It didn't take her long to know right from wrong.

Claudette, we're all still so proud of you
you stood for something more,
you stood with sister Rosa Parks too,
she is now honoured as "the first lady of civil rights"
and "the mother of the freedom movement."
That crushed all segregated seating on buses.

Claudette Colvin, Rosa Parks, we thank you both equally
for being so upright and so bold.
As Parks wrote in her autobiography, there is always
more work to-be-done in the struggle for justice.
So it's upon me and you and all other peoples
that the Claudette Colvins and Rosa Parks
of this mixed-up world of hell
never stand segregated and alone again.

Let's all buy a bus ticket that says 'all aboard'
there is no difference between you and me
let's buy a bus ticket that says, 'I love you,'
therefore you must love me too.

Let's not cross swords and feel scorned
let us all follow in their courageous actions
and be forever transformed
that's all I've got left to say till the end of my days.

Dedication to Sojourner Truth: Ain't I A Woman

by Mark Andrew Heathcote

Truth be told, I am strong
I am not just a cook or a sower
I am willing to share this earth equally
I am ready to bear arms for what's right
I'll-pull-a-plough-like-an-ox-to feed-my-soul
and my brother and my sister
and "Ain't I a Woman."

Look, ain't-I-given birth to-bigger-ideologies?
Than to talk lazily about economics or politics
there is too much idealism without substance
truth be told, I am bored of all your empty promises
look at me I have fed and raised a child to be a man
and he has bowed his head to me as his mother
but "Ain't I a Woman."

Ain't I felt the suffering of a mule
with the weight of the world on its shoulders?
Ain't-I-picked the locks of hearts black as thunder?
And made them laugh-cry-teary-eyed?
Ain't I gathered the stars and placed them in your arms
and all I ask for is but to be your equal.
No, I ain't your duplicate darling
I don't even want to be your world.

I'm a woman who wants only to be heard-
I sell the shadow to support the substance
I peddle my photo so it can live on your shelf
but that's not what I'm about
I'm about pricking your conscience
to all manner of unjust abnormal anomalies
I have only the good scruples I was born with
no, I ain't your duplicate darling
"I am stronger - I am a Woman." That's my way of living.

Harriet Tubman
by Mark Andrew Heathcote

She carried those scars in her fractured skull
praying to God makes him change his ways,
she'd pray simultaneously for the improbable,
pray for freedom that of her family's always.

Her hair which had never been combed
stood out like a bushel basket, and it had saved her
when she was hired out: hit by a metal weight
she thanked the Lord and blessed her faith.

Her unrelenting master wanted her quick sale
'people came to look at me; he was trying to sell me.'
But, as such and such, no sale did prevail;
'injury had caused her a temporal-lobe-epilepsy.'

'She changed her prayer,' she said. 'First of March'
I began to pray, 'Oh Lord,
if you aren't ever going to change that man's heart,
kill him, Lord, and take him out of the way.'

She even prayed all night for her master's death
for her own liberty or death,
'if I could not have one, I would have the other.'
'Harriet Tubman confessed to a negro brother.'

The Lord answered: Brodess died a week later.
She ascribed to visions revelations from God.
'I was a stranger in a strange land,' she said later.
When she escaped into her freedom's esplanade;

Tubman travelled by night, guided by the North Star,
when winter, the nights are long and dark.
Avoiding slave catchers, she said, in coded song.
'Farewell. I'll meet you in the morning, Mary

fellow slaves, I'm bound for the promised land.'

She carried a revolver and was not afraid to use it.
she made many journeys forth and back
to free other folk she always came in the winter
when nights were long and impenetrably dark.

When morale-sank guided by the North Star,
and when one man insisted on going back to the planta-
tion,
she pointed a gun at his head then said.
'You go on or die. I never ran my train off-
the track and, I never lost a passenger.

'I'm bound only for the promised land.'

Author Bio:

Mark Andrew Heathcote is a support worker for adults with learning difficulties. He has 200-plus poems published in journals, magazines, and anthologies both online and in print. A resident of Manchester, UK, he is the author of *In Perpetuity* and *Back on Earth*, two books of poems published by Creative Talents Unleashed.

She

by Ashu

She looked at herself
when she saw her image in the mirror
she saw that the mole
contained a whole and a hole

Saw that there's much to hold
in every fold

Many a time
the things that are said
aren't exactly told

Saw that a dent
can be a dimple too
and also that
one and one
are not always two

Saw that the greys
were actually the hues of life
saw that she herself
is her best ally

Saw that the extra ounces
don't necessarily pound heavy
saw that the cleanest, purest thoughts
sometimes look shabby.

Author Bio:

Ashu is an educator by profession and a writer by choice.
She writes on subjects near to her heart. She was awarded
'Master of the Word' by Philosophique Poetic International,
and her poems have appeared in several anthologies.

Rosebuds
by Mirai Amell

I packed
my past
in ripped rosebuds
and
let them
drift away

Those Days
by Mirai Amell

Those days
when I wander alone
crimson moments drifting
along a meandering stream

Those days
when I wonder alone
thoughts crumbling away
pulled apart by pain extreme

I wear my vulnerability
like a superhero's cape
invisible invincible
I am my friend

Author Bio:

Mirai Amell is a neuroscientist, currently completing post-doctoral research at UCLA, USA. She writes poetry in her spare time, as an escape from the cosy logic of science.

Fragility Cycle
by Jaya Avendel

Words born of my marrow and plasma
claim proudly their heritage. Once
she; my nemesis
the one I hold inside my heart and
dream about becoming
tried to rename a string of
letters I wrote in burgundy.

Burgundy, as in blood,
as in lipstick. I whittled the soft tip
into a ballpoint and
wrote on my finite skin in lieu of pen and paper.

The pigment is too bright for my
twilight complexion.

I am bleeding
bleeding ink I cannot contain
with nothing but adobe lace dreams to
remember myself by.

Author Bio:

Jaya Avendel is a word witch from the Blue Ridge Mountains of Virginia, passionate about life where it intersects with writing and the dreamscapes lost in between. Her writing is published in many online magazines and journals, and she also has publications forthcoming at *Humana Obscura*, *Green Ink Poetry*, & *Songs of Eretz* Magazine. Her work is included in print anthologies on women's empowerment and climate change. She writes at www.ninchronicles.com.

A Song That Invites
by N. Bertulfo

there is a song playing in the back
dew dropped into the pond
making every cell soft
like the warmth of a small palm

there is a song playing in the back
it burns lanterns in the night
it beats louder than your heart
to remind you when to fight

there is a song playing in the back
limbs drawing circles and arcs
light dancing off their figures
as they set off a wave of sparks

there is a song playing in the back
that sweeps the dust off the soul
that tucks you in the worldly cradle
and invites you to tap your toes

Wings

by N. Bertulfo

clipped wings don't stop me from singing
clipped wings don't shackle my thighs
as long as I can keep on kicking
I can fly, fly, fly, fly

clipped wings are still full of feathers
shades that only belong to I
as long as I can preen my reds and greens
I can fly, fly, fly, fly

From the heavens to the earth,
wings don't only take you to the sky,
so warm your voice, flare your feathers,
and
fly
fly
fly!

Author Bio:

N. Bertulfo is a writer currently living in California. She writes hummingbird cake, sometimes Devil's food, and bakes soap bubbles in the summer air.

Dancing With Ghosts
by Katy Boyer

there's a bar just around the corner from the edge of us all
where old wounds go to
linger gamble ponder drink flirt socialize fight and mostly
lie in wait
their enigmatic staccato conversation, married with wafts
of sobbing and the obnoxious, jagged
rin-tin-tin of music that never ever catches up with itself
tortures the very walls in perfect time to
the recklessly banging door and each breath the wind
takes
they wait for that smell sound sigh glance song colour word
flower sunset breeze taste light
that is their golden ticket to slide down through the
wormholes of our souls and cozy up to our naked
vulnerability as they joyfully rip tear so wide open
what we thought was healed whole forgiven released
we soak, defeatedly, in the warm familiarity of the shame,
regret, guilt and anger they present as if they bore
wondrous gifts of love
and so the cycle repeats
meditations, prayers, tears, the unbearable fear and
attempts at silencing the pain the anger
old tools and new tools are gathered assessed utilized until
the wound's bags are packed and with
all the love we can muster is blast down the river of time
where it bellies back up to the bar and lies in wait

but we grow, we bloom, we radiantly shine ever more
brightly until that glorious day when
that smell sound sigh glance song colour word flower
sunset breeze taste light beckon
the wound shows up
but in this peaceful most sacred of moments we do not run
the bath and allow it to set up home:
we kiss its forehead and release it to the Light

Circling Back to Truth
by Katy Boyer

my body literally vibrates joyfully these days
slow and steady like a full moon train you can rely on or a
sleepy cat's languid purr
the sun is courting my every cell with outrageous, strip-
me-raw flirtation
perfectly blue sky drips itself in between breaths to calm
my heart
render surrender beyond my comfort zones
WHAM! out of absolutely nowhere, just as the most
luscious wisteria I've ever met whispers promises to me of
light, love, adventure, my dreams coming true
stories show up like proud models on a Parisian runway
clad in wounds
I thought long gone
my neighbour stares blankly right in my eyes as I say "hel-
lo"
a dog somewhere howls relentlessly car horns blare
someone blasts insane music
and something somewhere inside me withers for a
moment: believes I am damaged
I overflow with gratitude as a righteous blast of warm wind
accompanied by
2 bluebirds who land right in my path pulls me back into
this moment
THIS MOMENT
I stop

admire a tree just beginning to birth to the brilliant leaves
she will bear 'til fall
I close my eyes
and breathe so deeply
life love the smell of grass the sound of the waves the
peachy taste in my mouth
and I remember: my body literally vibrates joyfully these
days

Author Bio:

Katy has been adventuring on the planet since 1964, which
has given her many opportunities to become intimate with
healing. This healing journey inspires her poetry.

I Am

by Monica Prem Bajaj

I am
dainty debutante of dandelion dreams
buried in the yesterday's dusk
never saw the benign sky of elysian musk
lamenting crimson scars of betrayal
soothing my 3am terrors by weaving moonbeams in
midnight portrayal
wounds veiled discreetly beneath skyscrapers of thoughts
intoxicated by consuming anxiety and solitude

I am
broken illusion of lambent lows
ennui hovers and doldrums flow at the core
chagrined at my own mood
thrusting vainly invincible lassitude
merciless memories etched on every wall
black night desires what white soul denies to haul

I am
Aphrodite yearning for amaranthine epiphany
inspiring my ink to write verses of scarlet symphony
my soul is tired of grey stains
fatigued of savoring blue potions of pain
desire to scribble surreal similes in each line
surrendering to fantasies and amorous rhymes

I am
Muses healing my heart by escaping in words
sewing tattered emotions with metaphors absurd
doing the patchwork of imagery over brokenness
giving sustenance to battered heart with sonnets
in hope, words may awaken souls at ease
breathe life in dead dreams
spread tranquil hues of peace

Author Bio:

Monica is a professionally trained educator from the North of India who uses poetry to inspire young people, and spread her message of positivity. She enjoys spending time with her husband and two daughters, and loves nature walks and music. Her debut poetry collection, *A New Dawn Of A Hundred Hues* was published in September 2021.

Booby Trap
by Kate Blake

as a well-endowed woman I attracted much unwanted
attention
most spoke to my chest, my face went unnoticed!
a grope, a squeeze or brushing against me,
it felt like there was no respect!

they jiggled and sagged and created much tension
for years I contemplated a reduction
but not really something I'd do
then one day I found 'the lump'

a check confirmed what I already knew
surgery the very next week!
nothing now to jiggle or sag or attract attention
no more bras or mammograms, a solution was granted!

although a rebuild would be cost-free
why would I go there?
it's other people's issue if they want to stare
I'm alive and very healthy with nothing to jiggle!

Universal Healing
by Kate Blake

no matter the issue
especially those requiring a tissue

my front line profession involved trauma
dealing with child protection matters,
abuse, violence and mental health issues
those war damaged, suicide, poverty, fears
and addictions ... injustices of every type

then on a personal level
family abuse, chronic menstrual pain,
relationships, broken back, breast cancer,
gas-lighting, sexism and bigotry
copped it in far too many ways ...

on a community/global level there are
wars, pollution, wanton destruction and waste
hypocrisy, inhumane treatment of others,
pressures of conformity and expectations, taboos,
plus all the isms that persecute and exclude

travel was a delightful geographical escape
often debriefed with kindly professionals
finding my spiritual path a natural progression
meditation became essential for my sanity
then poetry suddenly arose, what a cathartic

healer … writing it out, word play renouncing
all that heart ache, and knowing it was their
ignorance, not staged just for my sake alone

understanding we are each responsible for
every word, action and inaction eased the
turmoil in my heart/mind, balanced my
bewilderment that our world
was so harsh and unkind

as spiritual practice and meditation flourish
travel and professional help diminished
poetry the universal healing connection
thus establishing a healthy outlet
eases my emotional and mental upset

Author Bio:

Kate Blake (aka calmkate) has published poetry, fiction, short prose and photography in online literary journals. She shares her love of nature through her work, which is often concerned with meditation, personal growth, and the healing power of poetry.

Loud
by Susi Bocks

> kept down
> held back
> filled with fear
> and rage
>
> despair at every turn
> me, an unwilling victim
> blockades to stop me
> turbulence swirling me about

My history embedded a lack of power in me.
Years of criticism, critique, and disgust took its toll.
Thick layers of neglect crusted over on this shell of me.
Defeated, ignored, and scared.

But I dared to feel more important than what the day
rolled out.
I fought to experience life exquisitely, with the volume on
high.
Determined to engage with this existence full of substance
and force.
I clutched myself hard and pushed forward to lean loudly
into my future.

Not gonna hide from it anymore.

My Self Evolving
by Susi Bocks

my life, this winding and criss-cross journey
enduring the setbacks nature often offers
forces an accounting of my true self's mission

while I critically reflect within my soul
the revelation – the person I see in the mirror is not me
it hurts that I've lived with this stranger for so long

I vow…

no more continuing to plod along how others want me
I'll take the reins now to forge paths more to my liking
my destiny means claiming my glory and being wholly
present

Author Bio:

Susi Bocks (IWriteHer.com) has self-published two books
- *Feeling Human* and *Every Day I Pause* and produced *The Sound of Brilliance* as Editor of 'The Short of It.' Bocks has works published in many anthologies and literary magazines. She was a Pushcart Prize Nominee in 2021.

I Was, I Am
by Pallavi Baruah

born free, but with hands tied,
choices forcibly snatched,
trapped and owned by
a veneer of what appeared as love
dispossessed of me and mine

the thumping sound of the heart
like gavel being struck, sealed my fate,
pulverising everything I thought I knew
to ashes and embers, and yet
I rose from a vapid unknown,
re-born, re-built, re-wired, re-loaded

this bruised and quarried mountain now
stands transformed into cimmerian undulates
a gaping canyon of lost trust, forevers, promises,
only carrying within, orphic melodies of me,
intangible, unreal, existing as an idea
wrapped in stillborn and unborn wishes,
undressing poetry forever

A Calm Ocean
by Pallavi Baruah

like a calm ocean on a warm night
with zero shades of virtue & vice

I watch the sun set,
jaded with billowed sighs of longing

my stillness triumphs over my chaos
my calm embraces my storm,

restlessness finally turning restful
whims disappear with the sun

leaving me a museum of unshed tears
as I become that calm throbbing ocean on a warm night

Author Bio:

Pallavi is an incidental poet and a writer who embraces the
sheer joy of self-expression that poetry offers.

Wild, But Still A Flower

by Christine Bolton

I am wild and not like you
I am not elusive or rare
but omnipresent
to be found
everywhere you look, if only
you would really see me
in the grass and between
the cracks in the pathway
of your life

Overlooked and annoying
I grow where no one expects
me to flourish, because I can
pretty and yellow, like the sun
strong and resilient
multiplying in numbers
and sometimes overwhelming
my appearance
not always welcome

Yet, when noticed I am pleasing
to the eye for my brightness
but do not always belong
in another's vision of beauty
if left alone, my life cycle
would ultimately give pleasure in
its transformation

To be plucked and played with
soft lips gently blowing
on my lightness
sending me in a million directions
giving joy with my ability to fly
and granting wishes to those
who would ask, allowing me to
entertain for just brief moments
before being born again
and try once more for happiness

Enough Is Enough
by Christine Bolton

The white rose petals, dried and flat
lay between the pages of their book of life
memories of the brief periods of peace
lost in the surge of turbulent
and ever-rising tides of their conflicts

The storms would subside
and seas calm once more
a truce called and treaties signed
the ravages of their war debilitating
to both the mind and spirit

Over time the view on the horizon changed
coming into focus with each bouncing wave
the images different, beckoning
injecting new life blood into old veins
gently pushing her towards new territory

Now her wings he can no longer clip
they are protected and invisible to the eye
the collar at her neck, once taut
eventually worn away from the
perpetual struggle to be free

Her liberty earned at a price
paid into the coffers of their history
her determination unwavering
her spirit he could not break
she had found her voice

Where he withered, she thrived
his weakness became her strength
her transformation intimidating
rendering him powerless
enough was enough and he knew

Author Bio:

Christine Bolton was born and raised in London and now resides in the US. She has been writing poetry since she was a child, finding it instrumental in guiding her through life's twists and turns. Her poetry has been published at *The Literary Yard*, Spillwords and *MasticadoresUSA*, and she can be found online at https://poetryforhealing.com

The Clay Woman's Destiny

by Ecaterina Petrescu Botoncea

Under this mountain, I came many years ago,
and next to this fortress tower,
led by the footsteps of ephemerality, here I came,
to build myself a house, a well, and a family,
here I came, to the happiness fair,
to bring flowers and talk to the rocks about bliss,
I came to serve hot food to the birds that suffer from
melancholy,
and to hit with the shovel against the slurry of uncertainty,
on the streets and into the homesteads where mothers are
lulling their infants to sleep,
and under the nocturnal lookout of the centuries that have
become history,
here I came,
to become a mother myself and shape children out of my
own fresh clay,
but the stone inside the clay did not want to laugh,
the walls become of glass, I am a fish inside a fish tank,
from here I look towards illuminated crypts,
from far one can hear the tankers,
the silence is hiding to become…certainty,
and I have become blind from the brightness of harmony.

The Woman's Soul – A Song in The Sand
by Ecaterina Petrescu Botoncea

Of all the chemical shapes of my soul
I love chimera, sunrise and sunset the best…
then there's the haze rising above the time
the iridescence of the moments in the scent of a rose,
the bliss of climbing towards the last day in the calendar
and the tea offered by a bedouin
when you've stepped on the edge of the sand
in the hourglass…

Author Bio:

Ecaterina Petrescu Botoncea is a Romanian doctor and author of poetry, prose, essays, aphorisms, and travel diaries. She has authored several books, including *Camino*, *The Way to the Light*, *Anunnaki* and *My name is You*.

Today, She Has A Name
by Rashmi Buragohain

Here she is, sitting by the open window
letting her eyes wander as far as they can go
she knows not where to begin
she knows not what she would write
but she knows, her tears are too precious
to let them, just in vain, to flow
but today, she has a name and she has to grow

Eleven winters have gone by ignorant of her self
but today, she reaches for the kohl
she searches the drawers for those anklets again,
left somewhere forgotten, unwanted, unloved,
she messes the neatly folded dresses, left untouched
she wants the red one to hold her, desperately,
to allow herself to feel love all over again

she wants to feel beautiful once again
she wants to feel the breeze once again
those words still hammer fiercely
they still echo ruthlessly through the quietness of time
no Ganges would ever wash away the hurt hurled,
and could never undo the moment when it was blurted,
"You are the greatest mistake ever made!"

Resurrection
by Rashmi Buragohain

Ten years of cimmerian darkness
she lived through, breath by breath,
to let the smoldering sun smile

Draping the scarlet scarf so fiery,
the sun kept her quiet words crisp
while the svelte night sang a lullaby

Caressing the lonely, parched soul,
the night spreads a lilting melody
ushering the arrival of the distant zephyr

Resurrecting a dead poem after a decade,
the soft breeze cradles the long silences
to let her grow beautiful and to shine

Author Bio:

Rashmi writes about love, relationships, women's issues, and children. She has had several poems published in newspapers, magazines and blogs. She lives in Assam, India.

Rashmi holds a PhD from the Gauhati University, Assam, and she is an Assistant Professor of literature in a local college.

And Shadows?

by Francisco Bravo Cabrera

A glance of anger at the shadows that dance about her
room
and she longs for the embrace that haunts the air.
Patient...like a saint...she looks outside, through the window at her side,
and sees a grey parade of faces floating by.
Who's there? Are they dancing in a minor key? A waltz?
What's this I see?
Are shadows now of flesh and bone?
Perhaps.
Yet indifferent, and smiling, they passed on by beguiling.
At once she summoned white-hot suns to melt the burning
icebergs,
so that her ship can sail the night winds while the waves
struggle behind her.
And like her legs, that tremble while she walks defiant
down that cliff of long ago,
where old memories are anchored, like the smell of children's laughter,
or the image of red teardrops on the sidewalk,
she feels the strength that builds up fast inside her.

No longer ruminating in the anger, the gift of shadows, the
result of silence,
she reclines upon her bed of thorns and smokes the air
around her.

She lovingly embraces one last shadow, the face that broke
through that last wisp of smoke,
and then the music stopped.
And the dance suddenly ended.

She knows the wisteria no longer reaches her window like
before,
the old vines that brought her lonely fugitives with carni-
vals of fantasy,
and ghosts that mock the sunrise.
She's closed that door behind her…
And shadows?
She knows that they still dance in other people´s bed-
rooms filled with smoke…

Author Bio:

Francisco is a writer and an artist from València, Spain.
His artwork has been exhibited in Europe, Asia and North
America. He shares his poetry via his blog VALENCIARTIST,
at *MasticadoresUSA* and at Spillwords. As of 2019 He oper-
ates his studios and galleries from Omnia Caelum Studios
València.

The Hundred-eye Chest
by PS Conway

the hundred-eye chest gathers dust
in her attic of memories;

once each drawer shimmered with shreds
of her soul, sorted and separate,
each its own aspect, yet stored safe
within the whole of her being;

now the chest bides, weathered with age
each drawer peeling, gray and decayed;
no light issues, each drawer a sleeve
in a crypt of her dreams, betrayed

by the labels written by men,
formed from a pen ordained by gods,
emblazoned by pain and disdain
to restrain her parts from becoming
the whole;

in her attic of memories,
the hundred-eye chest fades away.

Evils of Curiosity
by PS Conway

gift from the gods
gilded misogyny
awaiting
Pandora's wrath

evils of curiosity
freed in infamy
framed by men
as deceit

to subjugate
 - - to make.... less
woe to man
wo-man

un-gifted shame
absent reciprocity
yet through all - -
hope remains

Author Bio:

PS Conway returned to poetry in 2020 after a long hiatus from writing. Since then, his words have attracted an ardent online community of readers. His poetry has been published in numerous anthologies.

Erin

by Eric Daniel Clarke

I'm confused to be honest,
I thought we were quite happy and moving along,
then it all got a bit miserable,
I was about to go to bed, I guess I'll not be sleeping yet.

You say you have missed me,
yet shown no sign of wanting to talk,
don't you see the mixed signals you're sending,
you went not me, I don't want us to keep being like this.

It throws me every time we stop and start,
every time you come back you blame yourself,
when you go you blame me, you'd feel the same
if I did this to you, never knowing where we are.

I'm sorry you feel like that,
no, I've not been stringing you along,
I thought we'd have met, it's just not happened yet,
I don't really know what else to suggest.

I'm not sure I can give you what you want,
yes, I want you to be happy too,
no, I'm not perfect, I have my faults as you,
it's taken a long time, sleep well, I believe we will.

A Beginning of An End
by Eric Daniel Clarke

A butterfly in the classroom,
a window-dressed reflection
of another bound by nature,
wings held, seen, yet silent.

No words, not asked, as if,
clocks tick, inside, out now,
shoes kicked off, barefoot,
a painted lady in her head.

~

He told her of an odd sock,
she said the loss is yours.

He told her of a loose thread,
she said she'd sewn before.

He told her of a collar worn,
she said should now be torn.

He told her of silver lost,
she said you bet no more.

He told her of an old cock,
she said had long enough.

He told her, nothing heard,
she said to silence, mourned.

Author Bio:

Eric Daniel Clarke is an Englishman, raised in the West Country close to Hardy's Wessex. He worked for many years as a scientist, and more recently began writing poetry and prose. His first book of poetry *Shorts: A Take On Poetry* was published in 2020. As @EDC_Writing his work can be found on Twitter.

Education: My Strength
by Asha Chauhan

A woman of vast erudition
applauded by one and all
always wore flawless public facade,
to veil her excruciating pain.

Her married life full of mournful aches,
hubby a total sleaze bucket, she no better than a manne-
quin,
in catacomb cold relationship.

Wretched and crestfallen,
laid crushed under avalanche of thoughts,
family pressure,
fear of society.

But how long could she tolerate?
Her suffering took the shape of a volcano,
pent-up emotions unleashed,
quietly she moved out of this stifling bond.

Using education carved a niche,
healed ugly scars,
now freely soars as a lively bird,
with variegated plumage.

Proud To Be Born A Girl
by Asha Chauhan

I am born a girl,
is this a crime?

Since birth society left no chance,
to clip wings,
demotivate and bruise,
by arrows of gender biases.

With trust in self,
my untamable soul,
dared to dream,
and shine like the Sun.

Shedding chrysalis of orthodoxy,
emerged as lively butterfly,
mettlesome spirit rose like Phoenix,
from ashes of shattered dreams.

I am my own master,
crossing impediments,
prove mettle and,
fight for right.

I am born a girl,
is this a crime?
NO, NO, NO

Author Bio:

Asha Chauhan is a social worker & an educator with a passion for writing. Her poems are published in various Army journals & school magazines.

Sometimes, in The Summer
by Andrada Costoiu

Broken arguments proved to be conclusive.
A further turn of the screw,
sealed the suitcase,
while I was still shining the shoes to follow my dreams.

I had no choice but go,
recover the grace,
since there was no return to innocence.

The bastard character of my novel,
who sold himself to every cause,
transplanted into a narrative from afar.

I do not miss the gossip columns,
bad critics of my time,
their pyres were sclerotic, lit in ignorance,
meant not to burn the villain but the truth.

Page after page I've written my own story,
filled with thousands of Nothings and thousands of
Everything,
that do not realize perfection,
but it's life.

Departure is a paradox,
at times is loud, at times is silence.
at times it innovates, and gives you knees to pray....
and sometimes, in the summer,
it gives you fields of flowers,
over the ruins of a past you climbed,
to get to where you are today.

Author Bio:

Andrada Costoiu has published works in the field of politics, on immigration and identity issues. Her work has appeared in the *Journal of Identity and Migration Studies* and also in a volume published by Cambridge Scholars. As a literary author, she has published a collection of poems, *Love poems: Insights into the complicated mystery of love*.

She is also the author of *Under the Iron Curtain*, a novel set in communist Romania and published by Niculescu Publishing House, Bucharest in July 2021. She blogs at: a-passion4life.com.

The Last Woman...

by Camellia

The Last Woman, as if a runaway from a lost tribe...
She stands by the edge of what she calls her earth...
Unseen, unknown, her kind... Her words, written in the
blood of broken conventions...
Surrendered by her side, Odin lays...
They say, there's no such thing anymore... A woman...
All that remain are statues, built in their name...
Better locums, like columns... Yet there she stands, in front
of the eyes of the blind...
Nearby, Lady Justice smiles with her blindfold opened...
Oh, but today, Odin weeps... His tears, collecting by her
feet,
like a prayer without a destination... For today, she wraps
her tongue, in the strings of a puppeteer...
Hades' kiss, a misdeed, just a single pomegranate seed...
Her words, a flying brimstone, a morpheme, captured by
Stockholm syndrome,
bound in her own chains, she collapses atop a "Him",
till the song of an immured nightingale, entwined in twin
fate, reaches her cage...
Angel wings she sharpens... Cutting through his sentences,
she breaks free...

"Mother, May I Not?"
by Camellia

Schoolgirl, a nascent muse... Soft clay, she parts her rays
and breaks her white in two...
Callous reins, tears of rain... Virgins cry, yet the reign of
Peitho remains...
Forbidden from the temple of Leto, amongst the satyrs she
lays...
Green voices, imprisoned flames... Hands pulled, tied to
the kitchen she stays...
Tresses that slowly gray, days that slowly darken... Absent
laughter of children, stray astray...
Unsown by the Mother Goddess... Questions in her belly,
unborn... Barren, or aloof is she? Unknown...
Cherubic hands, never has she wanted to hold... The door
in her middle, isn't anyone's to open or close...
Hinges loosened, words that spill... Sobriquets, her sher-
bets... Sweet... Cold... Cut deep...
Androphilia and Moralities... And a conformist's gavel,
playing opposites...
Navel string bound around her waist... And a shackle,
chained to her ring...
The ribbon she cuts... Behind her, the metal she leaves...
Through the door, she flees...

Author Bio:

Camellia is a business and marketing professional who enjoys singing and writing poetry in order to escape the mundane realities of life.

GABRIELA MARIE MILTON (ED.)

A Tale of Two
by Joni Caggiano

into blue orbs I rest my lamenting heart now tranquil
white ravens cleanse my crestfallen and faithful soul
starlings reflect my warrior shield on cerulean skies
suffering fragile child, now limitless no longer hides

silent and rusty the barrel of dad's old pal, his shotgun
thick smoky tongues, memories of painful long fingers
slumbering in monster shadows amid timid raised brow
no doors or boundaries so what icy evils may happen now

fear lags discarding smells of piss, rum, and vile bodies
four EMTs put her naked thrashing form on a gurney
recalling kissing cheeks of a snotty foul unshaven face
helping to clean buckets of mom's blood beating in place

Woods and Beasts
by Joni Caggiano

even small horror bellows weary
this bedfellow I did not invite
no fairy tales or pleasure to reveal
stitch up my eyes, a dismal sight
day time as daunting as a livid sunset
ballerina dress torn to a shred
my snot into a couch, I would smear
pulls strains of hair off my head
afraid she would leave me at a store
pores bleed, how I yearn to die
fear swells like a black prickly thorn
monsters lurk close where I lie
their diet, liquid, one calling forth beasts
fear howls, wishing I was not born
old and tired in my teens, yet wise as owls
praying I will no longer be forlorn
dancing junipers and snowy cottonwoods
call my name in a woody braille
God smiles within a brow of a bright star
this will not always be my sad tale
only those that own sight will see my scar

Author Bio:

Joni is an internationally known and published poet, photographer, and author. You can find more of her work on her blog, https://the-inner-child.com - see her publications page (https://the-inner-child.com/publications) for a list of books, anthologies, magazines, and contests. As a surviving ACOA, Joni's blog is an effort to give back - she's a retired nurse and paralegal with a strong kinship with nature.

GABRIELA MARIE MILTON (ED.)

Calligraphy
by H.J. Cross

She woke
to the waft of life calling
of all the lives she had not yet lived
On
        Her
              Way
to becoming like calligraphy
in what had once been
a block script reality

Scarification
by H.J. Cross

If I never knew your name
I may have felt less shame
but…
I would lack these beauty scars
made of
        Ash
            And
                Art
the marks
which refined perseverance
in my heart

Author Bio:

H.J. Cross's work has been published in a wide variety of publications. You will find further examples of her work on Ello where she is a featured contributor, writing under the handle @hjcross_poetry, or on Twitter: @cross_hali

Finding Hope
by Sarah Connor

I won't give up on it.
I can't.

Kneeling in the mud,
I gather up the shreds
and tatters of my ripped up hopes –

all gold and green and white –

the lost and shining scraps of hope,
trampled, discarded.

I stitch, hands shaking,
a wobbly banner, wonky lettered,
mud-smeared and indistinct –
it's nothing much –

I stand up tall,
let it unfurl behind me –
foolish and fluttering –
and the sun catches it

and it shines

I Am A Woman

by Sarah Connor

I am not a woman who looks into mirrors.
I avoid my own gaze. I'm a woman
who buttons herself into her skin each morning,
a woman whose story is graffiti carved
into her flesh. I am a patchwork doll, stitched
out of meat and skin, my story scrawled
in scars across my body.

I am a woman who tries to take
each new day as a gift. I'm a woman
who leaves last night behind each morning,
a woman carving her own story into the stone
of every day. I'm patchworking, stitching
a life of joy and pain, my story more
than just the scars across my body.

Author Bio:

Sarah Connor is a Pushcart nominated poet writing in Devon, England. Her recent publications include Black Bough, *Irisi* and *Spelt Magazine*. She is a winner of the Angels and Dogs Poetry Project. Sarah is a regular host at dversepoets.com, blogs at fantasticmetastaticme.wordpress.com and fmmewritespoems.wordpress.com. She can be found on twitter at @sacosw.

Pruning My Garden
by Linda M. Crate

first they mocked me because
I was loud until I learned to swallow
my voice down and make myself
into someone smaller and quieter,

and then they criticized me for
my quiet;

I realized some people were never going to
appreciate me as I was so I decided that I
was going to be me—

not everyone deserved access to me
so I started pruning my garden,

they didn't like that either;

I learned not to care because boundaries
are necessary and they help keep me sane
without them people just take and take
until you have nothing left to give even to yourself—

I decided I deserved better, so I became better
for myself and for those who were with me in the storms
as well as the sunshine and never forgot my name.

Wasn't Going To Let Them End Me
by Linda M. Crate

in my most agonizing hours
with the words of bullies
circling in my head like vultures,
as I laid on the ground in tears;
hating myself and my very existence
a thought popped into my head:

I wasn't going to let them end me—

my magic, my voice
would carry on as a testament to
my power and my ability to rebuild
from the ashes of chaos on brighter and
more beautiful wings than I had before,

I would build a new foundation for
myself and use their words to build the
castle of my dreams so they could see
I have always been the queen even if they
didn't know how to appreciate my worth.

Author Bio:

Linda M. Crate's poetry, short stories, articles, and reviews have been published in a myriad of magazines both online and in print. She has ten published chapbooks, the latest being *Hecate's Child* (Alien Buddha Publishing, November 2021). She also has four full-length poetry collections and three poetry micro-collections.

As If...

by Corina Dimitriu

As if the earth
which I feel underfoot
would be the sky through which I float ...
Stacking dreams,
reliving moments,
I gather clouds
in bouquets,
I make hem to the memories
with butterflies,
I throw to the angels,
serene scarves ... your eyes ...
As if that wasn't enough for me,
I greet grief with a smile,
I pull the joy out of my tears,
I lock dreams in whispers,
I sneak images through words.
I'm dripping, shadow,
through the hell of every day,
Happy!...
As if my soul
floats shyly
through the heaven of your coming ...

I Will Come

by Corina Dimitriu

I will come back
with my love
gathered in whispers,
with my soul
twisted into a thread
of forget-me-not,
with all my passion
spoken in forgotten kisses
which outlines
the raised wing
on your knee ...
And I will ask you:
"Do you still remember the eternity
which sheltered our flight?"

Author Bio:

Corina Dimitriu is a Romanian poet and a preschool teacher by profession.

She published her first book of poems called *In the Too Late of the Moment* in 2014. Her poems also appear in numerous poetry publications in Romania, and have received awards in national poetry competitions.

Sappho's Moon
by C. Jean Downer

Harvest moons rise and leaves fall, bud, and die
for her, they say it is a duty, a mutual fulfillment.
She dreams in her room, alone, where tree-branch
silhouettes spread across the floor, creep up the walls,
this ancient limb tapping against the pane she closed
to a new chill in the air. It beckons her, like summer
lovers throwing pebbles, waiting for her to acquiesce.

A misguided fool who fails to see streams of unseeded
lovers visiting. Their embrace warms her, hand by
gentle hand. Her cycle begins a different end.
She throws open the window, crawls upon the gnarly bark,
slips onto a trifurcated crotch, down its solid trunk, and
plants among its twisted roots. Descending through malo-
dorous
earth, she embraces the changes within, preparing for the
light.

When I Am Reborn

by C. Jean Downer

Deliver me as a tree
in a deciduous cult,
unheeding man's conformity

where my rings grow wide
in a natural cosmic flow
and leaves and birds

come and go,
where my roots thrive deep
beneath the shallow,

yes, my love, bury me there
among the trees.

Author Bio:

C. Jean Downer is an emerging poet and fiction writer based in Surrey, British Columbia. She is currently organizing her first chapbook, *Limbic Disco*, and has published poetry in *Wales Haiku Journal*, *Failed Haiku*, and *tsuri-dōrō*. After teaching literature, composition, and Women's Studies in academia for over a decade, Downer now spends her days with her wife and their two daughters and writes full-time.

To Take Flight (Letter to A Daughter I'll Never Have)
by Miriam Descendres

The anguish of void
dizziness of all the first times
to fly they said...
from one sky as in another
fly; let go; you can

Why can't you see?
You are not alone
because I know how easy it was to say,
just aerobatics, some arabesques
feeling the wind like a caress
then letting go

Yes, I know there is the emptiness; the abyss.
Fly, they said
unfold, breathe, and the breeze will do the rest.
Take flight, they said

Break them; the chains
break them; those shackles
break them; the cages;
let them shatter in flights of shards

Fly, fly, fly
and never let go your dream
the only reason to live
is to fly....

Author Bio:

Miriam thought she'd lost her quill somewhere along the tortuous roads of life, as for a long time she couldn't muster the courage to share her words. Now she is letting them flow. You can find further examples of her work on Twitter @13rrance.

The Toaster

by Anna Dwyer

When I'm near you, I can't work the toaster.
You guide me through simple things
that I already understand.
You think, you feel.
That I am not very bright.
You might be right.
Others disagree and we shall see who proves correct?
When I'm near them, my mind is sharp.
We talk of dark and light.
Shadowy things with wings.
That would make you flinch and stand amazed.
That my lips, my convenient lips
could frame those words.
And my brain, that absent brain,
could, without strain articulate such thoughts.
So, what to do with him and you and this sweet choice of
two?
Raise a toast of course to fear.
Which guards and hides emotions dear,
and yet betrays with each salt, soaked tear.

Music
by Anna Dwyer

I have a harp
which I can't play.
And one day,
those strings of notes might make sense.
Like innocence.
Gone away.

Author Bio:

Anna is a Brisbane based poet who has been published in
Orbis and as part of the Anthology, *The Poet's Quest for God.*
She has degrees in Literature and Communications and Ar-
chaeology from the University of Queensland. She works in
a supermarket stacking shelves and sometimes plays the
harp badly. She is bipolar, and describes living with this
condition as 'a bit like a constant game of snakes of ladders.'

Autoimmunity
by Mariana Dynasty

Away,
I stayed awake,
haunted by demons of doom.
Sleepy, yet my eyes couldn't close.
Tired, but my back blew heavy trumpets.
I whimpered in pain and ache. Hopeless.

Tell me, tell me quick.
For drowning is better than this drama.
How does a girl survive against women?
How do you win a battle against the trusted ones?

It took a million shields,
and no arrows to attack.
Like war against a contagious plague,
stayed out of their way,
and found my path.

You Kissed The Life out of Me
by Mariana Dynasty

It was dark,
deep in the middle of Tuesday.
You crept in,
smiling slyly and asking for help.

You said the work was too much,
and I was in the perfect place.
You said it would be better to stay.
That tomorrow was not so far away.

Seconds, minutes,
I could feel your gaze on my lips
closer,
you pulled my waist and swallowed my being

The memory of your breath makes my steps falter,
I breathe hard then stop to recover.
I try to run but it doesn't matter.
You are alive, and I want this to be over.

Author Bio:

For two years now, the author and poet, Mariana Dynasty, has been blogging at poemsofmariana.com where she posts poetry. She recently published her first book *My Mom's Shadow*, on Amazon.

A Master's Touch
by Jeff Flesch

I sit under a daffodil
and think about my mum

and all the other places
the women in my life came from

starting with not much
while loving with a master's touch

a steely determination and fire
learned to me

I see

petals of everlasting grace and guidance
falling from the trees

while I continue to be, the love delivered to me

Scents and Aromas
by Jeff Flesch

love lingers in scents
and aromas filling the mind

taking precautions out of the ordinary paradigm

creating shells out of dust
we creep along the coast
thinking more, feeling less

we redress —
socialization

relegating our needs to another field

along a road made of flowers
nestled in the broach
of our long-lost grandmothers' prowess

we kneel at the graveside, looking to the sky
for another aspect gifted to us

of the love we feel deep inside

Author Bio:

Jeff Flesch lives in Corvallis, Oregon, and was voted as the 2022 Spillwords Press Author of the Month for January and February. He is also a monthly contributor to two on-line publications, *MasticadoresIndia* and *MasticadoresUSA*. Jeff is currently in the process of compiling a debut poetry book, which will be published by EIF in late 2022. You can read more of Jeff's poetry at jeffflesch.com.

GABRIELA MARIE MILTON (ED.)

Wife of Lot
by Jessa Forest

How does it feel with a mouth full of salt instead of the languid, tamarind language of your city? The city that sings to you and you the only one who hears her.

What does she sound like? Soprano or alto? Silk or broken windows? Do the cries of the market slide down her throat like tamarind or salt?

Does the gutter water taste like gutter or peppermint schnapps or bourbon? What is your real name? The name you abandon as a wife?

I think I could live married to my city as the queen or live lost and alone with no one but my city to comfort me. I think you could too.

When you died, when your city died, you were looking at each other. What was that like?

After The Flood

by Jessa Forest

While Noah's sighs polluted the ruddy beach
littered with the bones of heretics,
their livestock, and other predators—

While He thanked God for the early warning,
the strong timber,
exclusion
from the slaughtered multitude—

the women walked around him like he was just another
corpse,
bobbing and rooting around piles of driftwood and soggy
cloth.

Picking out the useful things.

Author Bio:

Jessa Forest's writing examines the borders between my-
thology and reality, indulging in the gritty, visceral aspects
of speculative fiction and poetry. She has two self-published book series in circulation and her work has appeared
in traditional print and online magazines. In 2011, she was
nominated for the Pushcart Poetry Prize. She was born in
Arkansas, USA.

Untamed Eden
by Shari Foster

there was so much death
rattling me to my core.
there was no surviving that
quake. it shook every piece of
me lose. I floated away, my image
dissipating as though I were a fine
mist over a hot flame. that was
the end of the me that I made.
when I rose out of that hot hell
I was unrecognizable. many fled
my presence. I stood on a new
foundation. Solid. Myself. and
even those that returned, seeking
me, could not see Me through My
new mantle. they turned forlorn,
long faces set in dismay, and I watched
as they retreated to their own
illusions. Death is a fine thing. an
unwrapping of old tales. an
undoing. how hard we've worked
to create such a lie as one life lived.
I slapped myself so hard, I shattered
my own mask, unleashing the great
fire that had been smoldering beneath.
it was as though I were a god
set ablaze within an untamed Eden,

rotten apples strewn at My unsoiled feet,
and the echoing sound of My
own laughter as it charred the garden
back to the dust from which I came.

The Ravening
by Shari Foster

I had hidden away that beast
link by link bound in the dark
the "evil" of which I became afraid
how I once rejoiced in this rapacious
side of myself, as though
I be a saint in disguise
I could scratch and shatter away illusion
like mere reflections on glass
no lie ever withstood my claws
until I retracted them – or so I thought
the wolf will not be settled or stilled
no more than the lamb will fiercely protect
to deny the one, is to find the other
slaughtered in the field
only together will they be
whole and untouched
my untamed beast would have its ravening
be it me, or the world it freed
even in darkness its purpose would be wrought
again and again I felt its pummel
upon myself - ripping away every false façade
with its thirsty blood drenched jaws

Until Lo – We stood as One unchained

Author Bio:

Shari Foster is a daughter, a mother, a wife, an entrepreneur, and a passionate writer. These are a few of the badges she has chosen to wear so far in this lifetime.

Beyond The Veil

by Lisa Fox

light shines, filtered
through a
chlorophyllic matrix,
conning
my plant eyes. swaying
with hope,
rooted as static beckons,
I see
beyond moss crepe sheets
a place
where fresh air plays
beyond
algal curtains and
rank gloom.
the green mirror's
dispelled
shattered shards rise,
redeemed,
twirling in the bright
reborn

Fashioned Friend
by Lisa Fox

astray from anguish
poisoned by passion,
etched with existentialism,
malaise from malevolence,
pained by paternalism,
notched by narcissism,
carved by charisma,
regressed from rejection
erased by exploitation
bruised by braying banter
degraded with dirty deeds
i leapt -- hurtled
f r e e f a l l.......... to a
red puddle   clingy tar   pile of twigs.
pulling myself together
with a few spare parts left,
I fashioned a friend.
from blood and darkness,
a whispering shadow:
"fear no more."

Author Bio:

Lisa Fox, (pen name Jade Li) lives in Western Michigan, USA, almost directly across Lake Michigan from Chicago, Illinois. She has been writing poetry since her retirement from government work in mid-2018, and you can find examples of her work on her blogsite, Tao-Talk. She is a regular host at dVerse Poets Pub, and has had her poems published in the anthology, *The Anthropocene Hymnal: Songs of a Self-Defining Era* (Experiments in Fiction, July 2021).

Mother
by Jude Gorini

Brazilian woman and gold digger for others.
1995, racism, western hemisphere or just a land of liars?
One gay son, hundreds of heart breaks
thousands of heart attacks and that gunshot that melted
her heart.
"This is your past slave. Give him a son".
Cleaning old people's crap, washing their sorrow, smelling
their pain.
With alcohol she forgets; with Xanax she dreams; with tears
she destroys the future.
The drama is her.
Her wound spewed desperation hoping to kill her soul.
She prays, and I pay.
She cries and I die. What are chaotic thoughts?
Maybe a light... or just the bliss.
Nothing kills heart anymore, just that gunshot that
changed her forever.
I am my mother's wound, I am my mother's power, I am my
mother's future,
I am the hope running through her hands while
our blood destroys destiny
carving this peaceful present.

Author Bio:

Jude Gorini is an Intuitive coach, author and creative artist. He has published two poetry collections: *Words/Wars* and *Sorry, I'm mad*, both about his personal experience dealing with mental health, bipolar disorder and gender identity.

He has a podcast called "Healing with Jude" where he shares his life experience and healing tools with many guests from the holistic world.

Because of Me

by Gypsie~Ami Offenbacher-Ferris

You are who you are
because of me
I am who I am
because of her
we are who we are
because of them
they were who they were
because of all the women
who came before

I Am Not Sorry
by Gypsie~Ami Offenbacher-Ferris

You look at me with hate-filled teenage eyes, believing your
entire life rests on the decisions today.
Life as you know it will cease to exist and you'll never, ever,
ever survive it.

In your world I am the villain,
the monster that stands between
you and what you want.
In my world I'm your protector, your guide, the one who
loves you most.

I am not sorry.

Disavowing me as your mother,
a choice you have made.
I choose to teach and harbor you
anyway, keeping you from those
who would do you harm.

Heart wounded by those I loved most,
false accusations and loss of trust.
Breaking the bonds between mother and child, child and
mother.
Mother and Father.

I am not sorry.

Upon this bed where I lay now,
doctors and surgeons weave in and out pushing me to accept their care.
I decline choosing quality of life over quantity of time left.
This hurts you.

Into the veil of nothingness soon I will go, not as willing as
you believe.
Your angry words accost my pain-ridden self, begging me
not to go but, to stay. The balm of our tears soothes.

I am not sorry.

Up on that rock shining oh so bright,
I step upon as I follow the light!
He asks if I have any regrets,
anything that I wish I could change?
No, say I. I did my very best.

Author Bio:

Gypsie~Ami Offenbacher-Ferris lives in Southport, NC. Published in Cameron Art Museum's *Writers Respond to Art* Program, published in *Whisper's & Echoes,* an on-line literary magazine and in *50 Give or Take* for her story, 'Love,' also in *Visual Verse* for 'Mother Earth.' She received a competitive honorable mention for 'Abandoned Memories' in 2021.

Daybreak
by Ali Grimshaw

Each day a chance
for new green to reach us.
for listening to happen in a way
that has never happened before.

For air to clear.
And for us to come together
instead of apart.

For healing to blossom
forgiveness heard, shame shifting
to break the cycle of old chains.

For mirroring your love
revealing how your eyes
have seen me forward.

For rebalancing of Earth and sky
an atmosphere where all living things
breathe without fear of suffocation.

For dormancy to begin again
or throw off its covers
to jump out of bed.

For someone to return home
or find a home
or be welcomed to a home
for the very first time.

If You Are Willing
by Ali Grimshaw

How heavy is the thought forgotten
the thought one believed unpardonable.

It rides at the base of the skull
with strong pulleys that crank

the shoulders inward toward judgment
creating a corded neck of weariness.

If the thought could be remembered
if one was brave enough to want

to open it up like an old map
unfolding its tired edges

what could be changed by seeing
its landscape of the past?

Author Bio:

Ali Grimshaw contributes to the world as an educator and poet. She runs a writing circle workshop, where participants have the chance to experience connection with other writers and share the power of their own voices. Her poems have been published in several anthologies and journals including, Vita Brevis, *Right Hand Pointing*, *Visual Verse*, and *Ghost City Review*. You can find her writing circle offerings and her poetry at flashlightbatteries.blog.

Yes, But
by Jenny Gaitskell

I'm not the thing you think you see.
When you say don't, I've found me.

So, I wear odd frocks and laugh too loud, dance my own
can-can't. I travel alone touching myself wheresoever I
want. Daydream mouth open, every wish outspoken. Get
hairy, play unfairly. Change my name. Disclose my brain. I
begin starting again.

When you say no, I am free.
I'm not the thing you'd have me be.

Marigolds
by Jenny Gaitskell

mum's pink rubber gloves
pegged out on the washing line
stick up two fingers

laugh until we cry
these silly old photographs
taken by a liar

daily texts
sharing strength in single lines
mum sends back x's

Author Bio:

Jenny Gaitskell lives by the sea in Sussex, UK. She loves old dictionaries and everyday magic, writes speculative fiction, blogs on words and writing at jennygaitskell.com, and tweets poems and tiny stories @jennygaitskell.

African Woman
by Maropeng Florah Gama

Who is that African Woman with the smooth brown skin
Or should I say black skin
Who is that African Woman with the natural beauty glowing
endlessly
With the dark brown eyes glittering constantly
Who is that African Woman with the face preserving a smile
with the glamorous sound cheeks
Who is that African Woman with curvaceous curves
With a hefty staggering behind of which we call African
beauty
Who is that African Woman with infinite strength
With consistent hope with unfailing faith
Who is that African Woman with stagnant love aching abun-
dantly with unbearable patience
With slow motion pain appearing unshakingly
Who is that African Woman
You are that African Woman
I am that African Woman
We are that African Woman

Who Am I

by Maropeng Florah Gama

I am an African Queen
The heart that shows so much compassion
The beauty that possesses within, I am the future
The light that shines through others
The believer of heavens
The star which shines the way to others
I may not be perfect but I know I am a success
A dignified woman
With so much potential but little of courage, I am myself
With the soul and faith that can move a mountain
Any anything which seems impossible will become possble
Because I am the beating and living soul
I am a dreamer I am a visualizer
With so much talent but less of confidence
I am an inspiration which best suits the universe
I am an angel on earth which sees and thinks incongruous-
ly
With so much love worth death
But then I ask again
Who am I

Author Bio:

Maropeng Florah Gama is a female market researcher in Johannesburg, South Africa. She uses her writing to find a sense of healing and relief through self-expression.

I Won't Be Silenced
by Cindy Georgakas

My hands have tilled the rich soil of the earth, bound by chains and shackles.

Ghosts move under my feet hearing voices that were silenced.

The temperatures rise as the heat scorns my flesh, torn inside out,

where all humanity can see.

Dignity stripped to the core, lives burned at the stake, for no rhyme nor reason,

while my voice screams in vain. There's no rationale, and I won't be silenced!

I stand for one and all.

Tortured and twined with worry and anxiety, the roots of my ancestors bleed.

Smothered and suffocated as twisted minds strangle innocent lives, ripping babies from

their branches, longing.

I've died a million times, and been reborn a trillion. My echo rings loud and clear

and won't be drowned by political arrogance or greed.

Yes, I Am Woman and I will not return to being sold and compromised.

I stand on the mountain bluff and call my name and yours.

Let freedom reign

if not today,

then when?

Someone Saved My Life Tonight
by Cindy Georgakas

A prisoner of my mind

I walk the desolate streets, full of noise.

The dark cloud looms and has taken me hostage.

Wherever I go, there I am.

There's no escaping, wrought with compulsion and fear;

the radio sings, Someone Saved My Life Tonight.

I fold my hands and smile and say please and thank you.

My exuberance and beauty is polished, so you won't notice,

I'm dying on the inside, looking perfect on the outside,

and keep these voices, a prisoner at bay.

Sleepless nights and desperation take its toll.

This hell hole cell housing spirits as their DNA, controls my brain and soul.

143

I awake to the same nightmare everyday, drowning in a cesspool sea.

I cut the cord and fled. It doesn't happen all at once, drowning takes its toll.

Time moves slowly counting every second, minute, hour but the sand finally touches my toes.

This disassociation of a fractured mind, finally awakes to freedom and

Someone Saved My Life Tonight

and I thank the stars

it's me.

Author Bio:

Cindy Georgakas lives in Woodside, California, 40 minutes out of San Francisco. She is a Health and Wellness Specialist, Life Coach, Yoga teacher, P.T. and Craniosacral Therapist. She is also a monthly contributor for *MasticadoresUsa*, and has been published at Spillwords Press. She is working on her first book *Putting your Dreams into Action* which will combine her wit, wisdom and poetry in one unique volume, to be published by EIF. You can read more of Cindy's writing at uniquelyfitblog.com

Desperation
by Swarn Gill

sharp words larrup
he loves to scare up
attention
build the tension
everyone is on their toes
& she never knows
when the arrows
will fly at her

all those years
cement her fears
but she slings fierce
against her giant
non-compliant
so defiant

while blinded
by her tears

always
always he is peeling
love away

always does he
leave her
in a state of

disrepair
stripping
her parts away

always is he
removing a leg
from her table

always is he
redrawing the map

always does he lay
the barbed wire

& always
does she find herself
when she holds her pen

Sorority Sisters
by Swarn Gill

their life distorts
in a blossom of bruises
fingers glide
across welts
wincing

a stretch reminds them
of broken bones
never fully healed

they know the look
fear
shame
guilt
in each other's eyes

bonded in pain
so many
hardly a minority

alone & not
in their sad sorority

147

PTSD
by Swarn Gill

a door opens
fear-conditioned
is it him?

she gazes
out windows
worrying
forgets about food

hunger pangs
can't be sorted
from stress

afraid to shower
& miss sounds
while naked
& vulnerable

yet wishing
to hide away

from it all

as she waits
for the next
hammer to fall

Control

by Swarn Gill

time measured
for every task
to step outside
she has to ask

always her fault
never the winner
told
what to make
for dinner

shopping chaperoned
begging for money
cast as a grump
never a honey

cut away from
sister & brothers
no help is coming
hope is for others

Author Bio:

Swarn was born in Canada and grew up with a love of the weather, despite the punishing cold. He went on to foolishly go to school for many years to become a meteorology professor. Then one day he remembered he loved to write poetry and decided to do that too. Swarn is a humanist who is inspired by many subjects including inequalities and injustice in society, feminism, and the wonder and beauty of the natural world.

Meek As A Lamb

by Wendy Gent

meek as a lamb
she never says a word
that shy girl
but at night, under attic lights,
how furiously she types

Autumn Leaves

by Wendy Gent

late season fruit
in its prime —
she knows who she is now
youth, with its fear, cast away

Author Bio:

Wendy lives in North Bristol, UK, and has had a long career in financial services. She recently discovered and became fascinated by Japanese short form poetry. She has been writing haiku and tanka poetry for around a year, and shares her work on Twitter: @WendyGent_ She is married with two daughters and two granddaughters.

Note to Self
by Elizabeth Harper

I will no longer sacrifice the pleasures of life
to become who you wanted me to be.

Instead,

I will become what I want.
I will become who I need.

I will become...

Sincerely,
Me.

I am torn between
continuing the scorn
or becoming reborn.

The ultimate fight
between heart and mind;
the cruel compromise
between I and I;
the true meaning
between death and life.

But if only a name...

Then I am the torn.
I am the scorned.
And I will become

The reborn.

Author Bio:

Elizabeth Harper is a 26-year-old poet from central Oklahoma. She began writing poetry privately as a coping mechanism after losing her brother to suicide in 2007. Towards the end of 2020, she joined the Twitter writing community and began sharing her work publicly. In the span of one year, her poems have been published in 7 anthologies.

The Woman

by K Hartless

Drop earrings, droopy breasts;
everyone invests in the woman.
Heels heightened, centerfolds;
everyone's frightened of the woman.
Drill bit arms, collarbone bowl;
everyone farms and hoes the woman.
Mouth worth dismissing, milk carton calves;
everyone's missing the woman.
Slit of fine-grained slate, thighs that chafe;
everyone gestates in the woman.
Modeling clay, a man's property;
everyone tries to splay the woman.

A Period Piece
by K Hartless

The white of the sky blends into the thighs
of the bobbling, blubbery ocean.
It's her time of the month,
and she is bloated with clouds-
rocks like areola lie sore among her shore.
This daily flow of rain, a burden to bear,
but she must keep pace and force out air.
Winds to push the sails of men casting nets,
mirrored in their labors are hopeful depths.
Winds the waterfowl need to rise
make their treks, and dive to take a prize,
a flash among the cramping waves.
Her voice soothing the crash of rocks,
the wagging of sharper tongues,
but in her expansion, the sky never complains,
knowing it's just not polite to talk of such things.

Author Bio:

K.Hartless is a traveling writer with a passion for penning poetry, speculative fiction, and fantasy. She has been published in *Luna Station Quarterly*, *Visual Verse*, and *Last Girls Club*. When she's not editing her upcoming novel, *Fascination*, she is teaching writing and literacy in the Washington D.C. area. Her blog, Yardsale of Thoughts, offers bizarre treasures for readers to explore.

Woman of Substance

by Madhavi Hingorani

Don't you dare call her the weaker sex
she is anything but so
born with a skin soft as a petal
within her a resilience
that can crack a stone
don't be fooled by her tough as nails attitude
she needs to veil her compassion and benevolence
to survive on her own
in this male dominant suppressive society
history is proof of the
atrocities against her
condemned many times, in the name of religion
she has been burned by their acidic violence
but they couldn't break her spirit with their diktats
she walks with her head held high
her emotions like the moon
bringing the certainty of tides,
hope resting on her shoulders
her lowered eyes holding dreams
of a world without restrictions
she has mastered the art of
bouncing back every time she is pushed
rising from the mound of her own ashes
as gracefully as a Phoenix in flight

Her

by Madhavi Hingorani

They broke her to bits
crumbling her self worth
destroying the radiance she carried
mutilating her zest for living
ignoring her cries for being loved
she slept with demons every night
they stripped her naked with their
despicable hunger
feeding themselves with the blood of her soul
she was battered and bruised
from outside and within
and then someone came into her life
Someone who knew her like no other
someone who always stood by her
supported her through life's harshest battles
silently waiting for her
to come out of her own head
scraping off her dusty mindset
reminding her of her sass
why did she take so long to notice? Or realise
it was her!
She was the one she had been waiting forever for!
She was the lover she always wanted.
Her!

Author Bio:

Madhavi Hingorani comes from a family of travel aficio-nados and travel professionals. In 2019 she launched two blogs on WordPress: one related to Lifestyle (Aquagirl30) and the other to Travel (Tailwinds and Touchdowns). She wrote and self-published her debut book of short poems, *Hiraeth*, in December 2020. She lives in New Delhi, and can be found on Instagram @InkedbyMadh_v.

Lemonade Raygun

by Kim Whysall-Hammond

Born a girl so none of it
was mine to have back then
pretty things were bought for me
expectations placed elsewhere.
When I stopped playing with toys
I should have started playing with make up
got that factory job, stayed sweet and low.
Self respect is a lonely road and
others would not tread it
but I walked away head high
shot the stars with my
lemonade raygun.
Dad was proud but
she never forgave me.

Wilderness
by Kim Whysall-Hammond

I stand at a wooden lectern, heart hammering
as the large auditorium fills

My audience gathers
their eyes hunt me out, hungry for facts
as I delineate the close correlation
the dance together of world and time
how wandering satellites are innocent
betrayed by the planet beneath them
as it quivers and stutters
in its huge rotation

All this
hidden in passing milliseconds
until our orbital instruments
were not where we expected them to be
a millisecond here being miles distant up there

Entranced by this satellite pavane
my voice lifts in scientific song
the poetry of understanding
and joy of knowing
how the atmosphere can push
and the mass of the world respond

My speech ends to applause
and we drift to the bar
to talk numbers
I am home safe from the wilderness

Author Bio:

Kim Whysall-Hammond grew up in London, but now lives deep in the English countryside. She has worked in both Climate Research and Telecommunications. A late comer to publishing poems, her poetry has appeared in *Ink, Sweat and Tears, Bind Collective, Amsterdam Quarterly, Yellow Arrow Journal, London Grip, Crannóg* and others. She also has poems in anthologies from Wild Pressed Books, Milk and Cake Press, Palewell Press, Experiments in Fiction and Brigids Gate Press.

GABRIELA MARIE MILTON (ED.)

Heart Remedies
by Karima Hoisan

For the loves that were not loves at all
but pain and trauma, lies on lies,
who tried to cut the heart out of my chest
and left me in their dust, left me half alive.
I dip my quill into the little blood that's left
and dedicate a poem to each and every one
that I may not forget.

For poetry has stitched my wounds
the words are threads that bind
a verse that's written from a
broken, pumping, throbbing heart,
will stop the pain from spreading over time.
Apply the poem like a healing day and night,
take out your paper, pen and tears and
write and write and write!

Then when you want the scars to disappear,
so that you cannot remember, where they ever were.
(I know this to be, for sure), because I've done it once or
twice;
apply forgiveness, directly on the wound.
If it's sincere and if it's pure
one application should be enough, to last you all your life.

The Touch That Heals
by Karima Hoisan

To lovingly stand at bedside
of a soul who will soon depart,
holding their hand, spoon-styling them
taking away their nightmare
by saying, "You are not alone, I am here."

Let the pain-killers work,
to relieve their pain,
but you can relieve their agitation,
by touching them and show you care
stroking and soothing their hair.

Your presence is the touch that heals
even if they seem asleep,
clasping their hand in yours
you can lead them on their way
without anxiety or fear.

And when they take that last breath
and you feel them slipping from your grasp.
Stay strong, when it's almost too much too bear,
for both of you are being gifted,
the holiest moment you can share.

Author Bio:

Karima Hoisan lives in Costa Rica. Poetry is her passion, and she gives readings of her poetry on her internet stream as a performing avatar poet.

She has a YouTube channel: https://www.youtube.com/user/mistyshoressl and has been published at *Masticadore-sUSA* and Spillwords Press.

You can find more examples of her work at her blog, "Digital Rabbit Hole": https://karimahoisan.com

Go and Get 'M
by S.T. Hills

To unclose one's eyes on a day so bleak
wanting to shut them unable to watch
unhappy, dreary, unable to peek
laying under sheets, but feel the chill touch

You must rise and shine. Take control, be there
smile, nod, learn or teach, remember, repeat
do not give up, abandon hope, despair
keep on fighting the battle, slay the heat

Discard this unbearable poker face
you are worthy, such a beautiful soul
show the world that you belong, in this place
embrace life, have a purpose, have a goal

Step outside. Face your fears and conquer them
I promise, go for it, go and get 'm

Harmony
by S.T. Hills

Harmony, I desire such balance
Am I synchronized at all
Rambling thoughts
Memories twist
Overthinking
Needing
You

Author Bio:

S.T. Hills is a Dutch writer working on a crime series and has the following work published: *VSS365 Anthology: Volume One* – Published by Mark A. King *Crispy Rooftop Conversations*; *Hashtag the Horizon*; *Prompting the Moon*; *Poetry in 13 volume 2 & 3*; *Flashing Conversation Stories*; *Quintessential Universal Erotica* – Edited and published by Scott Christopher Beebe; *Catch me, I exist* – Published by Dawn Serbert- *FromOneLine volume 1 & 2* – Edited by Meghan Dargue and Published by Kobayaashi Studios

Dear Heart

by IA McCleery

Deep within her Soul,
completely out of reach,
beyond all understanding
unexplainable in words
she continues to rise above,
above the emotional disease,

Pushing through
the generational curses
that are too numerous to list,
addictions that have destroyed lives,
lives that had so much potential
so much worth, desire, and love,

And so she continues,
continues to Dream, to Aspire,
to Bloom despite the odds,

Let no one tell her
that she is almost there,
her surging energy
her passionate heart
is truly almost there,

So continue Dear Soul,
continue to blossom, to grow, to reach
for pure and complete healing
Dear Heart

Reclaiming The Light
by IA McCleery

Salty morning waves swallowing footprints
sprays misting grains of sand on the beach
echoes softly splashing ashore,

Her heart enveloped with hope
her soul passionately embraced
she is gifted another chance,

The brilliant rising sunlight
ensures another opportunity
to rewrite, renew,
recreate her own
inner light

Author Bio:

Writing under the pen name, IA McCleery, Angie is a Medical Oncology Coder by day and writer by night. She shares her poetry on Twitter, and her first publication is from the #InstantEternal prompt and includes three submissions accepted for the *In Frozen Prose book, Volume III*, 2/2022. Her work has been highlighted twice in the Twitter MoveMePoetry Weekly Battles since her submissions started in 2/2022.

Free

by Alexandria Johnson

the cork pressing down the bottled-up feelings finally
popped,
and overflowed after being restrained for so long.
I thought I couldn't fly when the baggage
from the past was anchoring me down.
but when my mom told me I could,
I stared into space trying to register
every bit of that information.
never in my life did I think that—that would be possible.
these feelings, trapped for twenty years,
are no longer trapped.
they floated high like the clouds,
drifted away in this air balloon, taking them far from me.
freedom, my conscience says, and at last,
freedom it was for me,
today I soar high in ecstasy.
tomorrow? we're not going there,
because today is a new chapter of my life,
to always keep discovering oneself, myself.

now, turn that page.

Author Bio:

Alexandria Johnson is a 25-year-old emerging writer and poet based in Malaysia. Her poetry has appeared in *The Star* local newspaper in conjunction with International Women's Day, *iRiS Magazine #1*, *The Poet's Haven Digest #4*, Spillwords Press, and Noctivagant Press. She shares her poetry on Instagram @alexwritesandsings.

Strength

by Esha Jaiswal

Abused
invaded by obsidian sorrows
I cried, I crumbled
my life turned upside down
ensnared, jumbled
broken from within
when swiftly
the light came in
this is my chance
I start to breathe
you want to let me down
but I won't give in
I pick myself up
piece by piece
soak my wounds
in hopes & dreams
I shall bloom
I shall fly
touch the sky high
dazzled, bemused
you look into my eyes
you undervalued my strength
and now, you know why

I've Healed Myself

by Esha Jaiswal

I'm defined by
little tragedies
that map the scars
embellishing my skin
I've survived
the collision
with moments of
'I don't love you'
sipping in
the troubled
wine of ache &
relishing
the taste of salt
in my wounds
I've healed myself
with oceans
and mountains
I carry in me

Author Bio:

Esha is passionate about poetry, through which she celebrates her love of words. She shares her poetry on Twitter
@EshaJaiswal19

Beginnings

by Jo Lynn Juneau

Cast out of Paradise, Eden's perpetual exiles
the surreptitious serpent, now lies crushed under our feet
God took a lesser part of Man, and created from it the
strength of humanity
we bear the world in our wombs, and bear its weight on
our shoulders
we suffer the pain of giving life, so we suffer death differently
we are harbingers of antiquity and the future
we are Goddess
we are Mother
we are One

Foreshadowings
by Jo Lynn Juneau

I sometimes see things before they step into light,
though I learned early on never to say
it frightened my mother; she said I had the devil in me
I never bothered to correct her, even at the insistent urging
of a Mimosa tree switch
now, I have learned to be grateful for the things I see,
and at times, even more grateful for those I do not
                    Mimosa trees…
I never again saw as things of fragile beauty,
but as a painful reminder of the wisdom in discretion

Author Bio:

Jo Lynn Juneau is a poetry lover and published poet. Her work has appeared in numerous poetry anthologies, and in several online publications, including *MasticadoresUSA*. She currently resides in the United States.

Between Two Ferns

by Sarika Jaswani

I roll hours on prayer beads
between drips of IV, hiss of ventilators sways your masked
breaths

Pixelated screen once had slimmed distances now fails to
meet the grudge for not holding your hands

Between much to say, unsaid
I yell 'I LOVE YOU' over and over again
reception fades—with your nod
palm folded tight on your chest

An indifferent year passes—

Through my window
ache rails a season
color to ashen

Over-plucked memory weeds
now sit seeded, deep in the dirt
waiting on rain

Doctors say your mother lived with an enlarged heart, died
breathless from a virus

Between two ferns—
I manage to suffocate the night
phases of my shrinking moon

Author Bio:

A doctor by profession, Sarika Jaswani is a crochet artist, art tutor, and writer. Her poetry has been widely published in online literary magazines and anthologies, including *Tide Rises Tide Falls*, *Fevers of the Mind Poetry*, Silver Birch Press, *The Organic Poet*, Spillwords, The Women Inc, *Trouvaille Review*, *Antonym*, *HeronClanPoems*, and *Synchronized Chaos*.

Petals of The Dead

by Annette Kalandros

I tossed them to flames
some time ago—
petals of the dead.
Some flowers taken
from above the six-foot holes
I stood over, freezing in emptiness
of an empty hole
about to be filled.
Some flowers taken
from birthday and anniversary
bouquets of celebration,
marking years of bitter happiness.
Most flowers taken
from a wedding bouquet
of vows taken, kept,
a reminder of vows abandoned.
Petals of the dead kept
out of wretched sentimentalism
I burned upon the pyre
with myself.
Then climbed a new self
of burnished bronze
from the flames.

Who I Am?

by Annette Kalandros

I tire
slaying demons,
not my thing—
I've chased
misplaced
braced
for the reckoning
of evil deeds.
I've offered up my neck
to bring utter happiness
and still—
nothing would do
till cutting myself in half
to dig, dig, dig deeper,
bury the self beneath the soil—
the dirt of need, want, desire
lay it all to rest in the infertile
grime, the level of your rule,
to be consumed by rot
of prayers you pretend to answer,
but you are neither God nor Goddess,
despite all your pretentiousness.
In this, this turning away,
I offer up prayers
to God and Goddess that truly be,
and I do lay down the sword

I used in battle with myself:
thus, I become the warrior
I was meant to be.

Author Bio:

Annette is a retired teacher who has been active in the LGBTQ community since the early 80's. She is honored to have her work featured in the following anthologies: *As the World Burns: Writers and Artists Reflect on a World Gone Mad*; *Through The Looking Glass: Reflecting on Madness and Chaos Within*; The Pinecone Review's *Be Proud with Pride* Edition and Survival Edition; *Women Speak: The Women of Appalachia Project*.

Finding Only Fog
by Tres K.

I thought I saw a ship come in
upon waves of Lake Michigan,
finding only fog rolling away.

Hang my head, shove off again,
low clouds of existential dread —
do we float alone here anyway?

Lighthouse blinks as shadows sink
and drag me underneath the deep
to realize a fear of dimmer fate.

Water saturates my lungs —
sometimes I do not cry enough;
salt springs to the surface none too late.

Surrendered to a turning tide,
I'd drift without anchor of pride,
dropping shame's unnecessary weight.

Currents swell in ebb and flow;
my vessel might not ever know
if her name sails far beyond the grave.

Perfection Realized
by Tres K.

Late at night, my anxious mind
extracts events from random times
and then inspects how they align.

To my terror, too often I find
the critic left unsatisfied ...
but then you sigh.

Snuggled to my side —
perfection realized;
the needless worry
and nonsense fear
suddenly
disappear.

Author Bio:

Tres K. is an up-and-coming indie poet whose body of work
has been described as lyrical and layered. Originally from
Flint, MI, she currently resides in a small farming community with her wife, daughter, and a pack of random animals.
You can find her words on Twitter @tysm_poetry, or connect with her during the weekly #MMPoetryBattle hosted by
@MoveMePoetry.

Choosing Myself
by Christine Kelly

Love,
unmarred by time or quarrel, is patient
and blind,
to red flags fluttering in the wind.
It's easy to lose yourself, be diminished
by another's perception and resentment.
Days turn to months, to years; you exist
moment to moment, hoping
if you try hard enough it will get better.
It never does.
When deeply entrenched in dysfunction,
finding a way through is gruelling, an arduous journey
fraught with grief and pain.
I'd been conditioned to believe I was incapable of anything
and deserving of nothing.
But a voice inside, quieted for years, spoke to me – I lis-
tened and took the leap.
I chose myself over security.
I chose myself despite paralyzing anxiety.
I chose myself, and in doing so allowed the woman within
to emerge.
Ready to create the world I needed to live in
Ready to be all I could be.
Ready to be me.

Dreams Take Time
by Christine Kelly

Dreams take time.
Every day is a course charted across unknown seas,
bringing me to the shore of realization.
The journey is challenging, often demoralizing,
sometimes we are blown off course.
I had a dream once – in retrospect, it was a dream full of
naïveté.
Little did I realize it would take me to hell
and back, with an all-encompassing desire
digging deep into my marrow – superseding every other
need I had.
I would have made a pact with the devil
to kindle that dream; nurture it to fruition.
Silently, pain and grief my constants, I labored in its service;
loss the only thing I thought I'd know.
Only after its fulfillment, after my world had crumbled, did
I understand –
I had to look within.
I saw myself for the first time. Not through rose tinted
glasses
or the prism of another's disappointment,
but an unvarnished appraisal of the courageous, flawed
woman I am.
Knowing my voice matters.

Understanding I am the only one capable of captaining my
own ship.
So, I set my course – adjusted my sails, leaned into the
wind,
and guided myself home.

Author Bio:

Christine Kelly is a poet and writer, currently living in Illinois, where she is often found scribbling poems on scraps of paper, frequently in church. Her work has previously been published in *Voice of Eve*, *Heron Clan VII and VIII*, and in Medium magazine's *PS I Love You* and *Loose Words*. She is currently working on her first poetry collection.

First Woman
by Alethea Kehas

You may call her Eve, but I know her as Melissa
first woman born of clay. Write her story, they whisper
and so I do, following the trace of her body
born supine to face the sun. My eyes watch the slow
unwrap of the goddess. A womb like a hive
pulls the drone of the mind anxious to follow pain
I turn back
relearning the slow unfolding of woman
and touch the mother-skin lifting its mold
so slowly I ache abandonment. Her form
the mystery I need to remember
how carefully she births self without division
and smooths the folds until lines become curves
until there is no beginning or ending
she just is

I Forgive You, Mother
by Alethea Kehas

I forgive you, mother
for giving the window your eyes
while your husband formed a vice on my throat
I forgive you, mother
for feeding lies to my imaginal cells
malnourished, the body is unable to make wings
I forgive you, mother
for haunting me like a demon-lover
searching for a fertile womb to seed your pain
I forgive you, mother
for letting water swallow my daughter's
breath while you wrapped anger in your arms
I forgive you, mother
for discarding your afterbirths like unwanted thoughts
six impossible beloveds buried under the feet of his throne
I forgive you, mother
for finding refuge in the abyss of your shadows
because inside your darkness, I have found my truth

Author Bio:

Alethea is the author of *A Girl Named Truth* and *The Labyrinth*. She finds home in the practice of yoga and in the wild magic of ancient landscapes. Alethea blogs regularly at "The Light Behind the Story," and believes truth is found through the exploration of the self.

Centuries Apart
by Tanvi Kamra

*Wrap the string around your palm and tug on the corset with
your might,
my muffled screams, they have no worth so I beg of you to
wind me tight.*

*These scarlet shades can mask the fear as I lay vulnerable at
dawn's call,
I suppress the screams as he smudges the scarlet and I hold
my shame as I fall.*

*That girl a century from now, I wonder if her words exude
her power or her pain,
does she uphold her own sanity or do the corsets still silently
block her vein.*

I hold up the shoulder pads and the briefcase with pride,
"Today is going to be better," I step into the world unteth-
ered from the fear I hold by my side.

But that pride soon slips into exhaustion as I inhale the
reality check just once more,
my shorter paychecks and their words I overhear, strike the
maim till it's sore.

That girl a century ago, I wonder if the world saw her
plight,

could she uphold her own sanity or did her husband's
shoulder pads suppress her out of sight?

All I had was myself but myself had no courage instilled,
if I spoke up, would they listen or just like my dreams, have
me killed?

I live in the reign of the queen and her power over the nation
we reside,
yet I have none, the power over my own house, nor the
guidelines I'm bound to abide.

That girl a century from now, I wonder if her land is her own,
the power that presides over the nation, I hope her struggle
to them is known.

When I scream for my right to abortion or they question my
word against his, I'm blinded by the nation's "glory",
the barricades along our inundating requests lead to the
eventual caskets of our unheard story.

Centuries apart, battles diverse, yet what's common is we
still combat the world each morning,
that girl born today at dusk, I wish she wouldn't read this,
I wish that she lived in a world where she needs no such
warning.

Author Bio:

Tanvi is a writer who tries to figure out the illusions of the world through her poetry. This poem is a contrast between the struggles of women who are communicating through two different eras. One explains her struggles as she lives in the Victorian Era and the other as she lives in the late 20th century.

She Is Perfect

by Naomi Karsudjono

You will notice when she enters the room... No, not merely
because of how she looks,
you will notice by the warmth she brings
that leaves a trace of delight resting gently into your heart.

She has that sparkle in her eyes... A twinkle of light.
her gaze, there's hope in there.
She believes everything is going to be alright.

She is a mystery... Not for the words left unspoken.
But for every word that flows from her soul,
a door opens to a new horizon.

She is present... With all her heart she is here.
Even though between her laughs, it's almost clear...
Her mind tends to wander into the future, far or near.

She is strong... Even if tears have fallen down her cheeks
and words have failed to escape her trembling mouth,
she is no less strong than she was before.

With all her vulnerability, she is strong.
With all her flaws, she is perfect.
She is perfect.

Shine A Light

by Naomi Karsudjono

Shine a light for every joke that was meant to be harmless,
but instead it ridiculed the presence of women.

Shine a light for each time a woman's deemed to be too
much, too emotional,
too sensitive for speaking up with her voice, for being true
to her heart.

Shine a light for each time a woman hears
"you're beautiful if only…"
"you're enough if you are less of a…"

Shine a light for each time a woman is blamed for the hor-
rible things that happened to her.

Shine a light for every finger pointed to a woman
with words of hell shouted to her ears and evil names
framed to her face.

When you shine, you shine for a hundred women who are
kept blindfolded in the dark
when you shine, you shine for a hundred little girls who
dream to light a spark

Author Bio:

Naomi lives a simple life with her family in a friendly town where everyone is glad to see you and the sky is always blue, Banjarbaru, Indonesia.

GABRIELA MARIE MILTON (ED.)

Hanging Liberty Walls
by Komaljeet Kaur

A scarlet sari draped around her waist that had some scars,
some visibly dark marks;
I wish not to compliment her beauty, her eyes drifted
towards dark, producing a gleam and then unanimated
sparks.
She wore a smile, that perhaps grew rustic with years,
a door behind her flung open, they welcomed her and she
greeted them with tears.
A chill climbing her spine on a hot day suddenly stopped in
between,
several eyes glaring at her from a dark corner looked indeed mean.
She picked up pace, soon, her heart was in her hands,
she destined to gear up her dreams; the encounter with
hazy figures was completely unplanned.
Her screams tore the silence around; their monstrous
laugh grew cruel and wild.
Her torn skin showed how cruel they were, the news reads
"Condolences to the half-dead child."
For some days, newspapers sympathized her, the agitated
nation too protested.
The Sun hid itself, Sky yelled with anger when they heard
another one being molested.
Our nation is progressing, we indeed are empowering our
women. Hurrah! cheers!
They gave me a count of hundred such women. I wished to

meet them but before dusk, they all disappeared.
I see, I see, how our women are empowered when their
safety is disgraced.
A man glaring his colleague quoted, "I can't help! It's a
matter of taste."
Yes, we are empowering our women deepening fears in
their minds more than before.
"Kalpana, Saina fades in front of my eyes… I can't be like
the women, I adore".
Her eyes shed tears, her lips still hesitated, "I deserve
respect the most."
"My eyes still hunt for the spirit that was killed, they won
the battle and I lost."
Hanging liberty walls, dignities being crushed
and freedom being challenged.

My Body
by Komaljeet Kaur

My body has the same set of humanoid structures as yours,
like an emotional pump, a brainless device and others few.
My body painted with pride and love, is sometimes soaked
in deep waters of shame and regret. The old gray concave
mirror in my room flirts with the Milky Way, tied up to my
ceiling and mocks me and my olive green body.

"This body of yours…. Don't you think is sluggish, a little
fat, slightly caramel brown, unfriendly and short? Don't
mind me though…. I believe it's a pure defective prod-
uct…"
The layer of skin melting under the hot merciless Sun
knows more lies, more tales, endless struggles of the past,
present and the future. This mindless female body has
heard a handful of handsome lies, bitter truths, disgusting
remarks and a two or a few lustful comments too.

The milky, slow moving fog delimits my supple body from
swallowing the blank space further and tries to ignite the
lost pride. My body speaks my mind. It's an art of surviving
not only hot and cold temperatures but also some arid
faces who conspire with my past to blur my smile. It's an
art of communicating with others when my hesitant lips
are sealed.
The poor body though has an extravagant dream of making a round trip to the moon.
"This is my body, my choice, my pride. Don't toy with it.

205

It's not an object to please others, or to withstand any kind of physical, mental, or emotional abuse, or either to sing glories for bruises hiding under the skin."

The caramel brown skin, a fat little body is someone else's ideal type.

Author Bio:

Komaljeet Kaur is a university student, who writes poetry at her "flavoured poetry" blog on wordpress. She uses writing as a form of healing and self-discovery.

Mom's DES Baby: The Hardest Pill To Swallow

by Barbara Harris Leonhard

I dig into the edge of grief. Unhealed betrayal.
Childless because of Mom, who never doubts
a doctor's word. She's spotting, fears losing me.
Is prescribed Diethylstilbestrol (DES). Blesses me

With a T-shaped uterus, infertility, cancer threats.
Tumors abound. Breasts, thyroid, uterus.
A pregnancy, possible, but not viable.
My deformed uterus delivers pain.
How can I cuddle
This bloody mass?

Mom is beset. To reassure her, I lose my need
for her hugs. Hold her grief in my broken womb.
Her comfort first. Does she see me? I sting of shame,
dismissed. How she forgets!

One day says – out of nowhere –
shattering words out of her scattered mind,
You're still childless? Don't know why!
I dropped seven!

I dig deeper. Uproot the past. Undergo major extractions.
Swallow the dirt - A total hysterectomy.
A partial thyroidectomy. All tumors benign.
Cancers caught in time.

Still, I grieve. My womanhood, aborted.
My eggs, dispatched as bio hazard.
My hollow earth. My barren feminine.
My broken lineage.

Now I'm "other," watching young mothers.
How they procreate. Carry their worlds.
The ecstatic births. The breast feeding.
All the sacrifices. All the stories.

Never a mother except to my own.
I'm her cane, her calendar, her brain.
My uncle asks, Do you love your mother?
My soul asks, Have you healed the wound?

Unearthing my trauma,
I swaddle my aging mother
to birth myself.

Ode to The Embryo That My T-Shaped Uterus Miscarried
by Barbara Harris Leonhard

You left my broken womb
as the bloody remains of what
was never to come. But I still feel you
in the waves, the flow
of my sacral river - your tears?

Your fears I've abandoned you?
No, Honey. No! I will never forget you.
The t-shaped womb
couldn't hold your brilliance.
Your tiny, beautiful self,

washed away. But your light
sparkles in each of my cells.
My core, your forever home.
Your essence, my creative labor
in verse and art.

Everyone says, Forget the dead.
But I can't leave my baby
screaming in her forever crib.
Or my young miss alone
in harm's way on grief's edge.

Though never delivered
into my arms, you shelter
in my wound of wanting. Each night,
I press my scar against a pillow
to swaddle you in your mother's heat.

In dreams, we share the sacred skiff,
and together, wind up and up
out of the wake
of the wound
into a newborn sky.

Author Bio:

Barbara Harris Leonhard's work appears in several online and print publications. Barbara won third-place and honorary mention for two poems in Well-Versed 2021. Her poem "Marie Kondo Cleans My Purse at Starbucks" was voted Spillwords Publication of the Month of January and February 2022. Barbara was also voted Spillwords Author of the Month of October 2021 and recognized as a Spillwords Socialite of the Year in 2021. You can follow Barbara at https://www.extraordinarysunshineweaver.blog.

The Life From Beyond Life

by Gabriela Marie Milton

After you died the city changed.
Its balconies turned upside down pouring dirt and withered roses on the sidewalks; blood coagulated under my tongue; a crooked sunset feasted on old walls like ants on insect eggs. A cannibalistic banquet that nobody noticed.
I screamed. The antichrist smiled at me from the left mirror.
I stepped on the other side of your death. My bones became yours. Your flesh became mine.
Metempsychosis.
Tongues of prophets locked inside my throat, eyes full of sand, lips sewed, chest open, my heart in my hands. Was it my heart or was it yours?
You looked handsome in the coffin. Why do they make dead people look handsome?
But it wasn't you. It was not even a copy of you. It was a copy of nothingness.
One night I dreamt a pair of new shoes.
The next day the city changed. It straightened its balconies.
It perfumed its roses. There were no ants anymore.
The 6am shower smelled of Love in White.
I covered the sea with my hair.
I anointed the earth with my lips.
You smiled. I understood.
At the intersection of Saturday and Sunday I was the life from beyond life.

Author Bio:

Gabriela Marie Milton is a #1 Amazon bestselling poet and an internationally published author. She is the author of the best-selling poetry collection *Woman: Splendor and Sorrow: Love Poems and Poetic Prose*, and the author of *Passions: Love Poems and Other Writings*. Her poetry and short prose have appeared in various magazines and anthologies. Under the pen name Gabriela M she was awarded 2019 Author of the Year at Spillwords Press (NYC). She blogs at short-prose.blog.

Fighting Back
by Sheila McGill

He looked down at her. He towered
whippersnapper, new to the job
trying to soft soap, but his words cut all the same.

New policy. He mumbled
hiding behind Covid cuts
it's not me ... you understand.

Forced Redundancy ricochets. Surprise gags

Smooth talking sucks all sense and devastation floors.
She was cornered. Legs had buckled
years of experience trampled beneath his ambitious intent

Down but not out. She gathered facts
Union gasped disbelief.
Strength summoned until finally, finally the grievance seen
sense

Justice makes one feel taller
today she is still there, but he is long gone.

In That Place
by Sheila McGill

Where the deep blue
dreams of being sky
she feels the weight of it

Pulling mood down.
Place of no return
gasping for breath

Seas of overwhelm. Drown
but look there
do you see her kicking?

Back

With all her might
searching for meaning
the glint of happy

She sees it flirting. Glinting. Dancing
above the surface, giggling with dawn's light …

Kick harder, kick,
kick.
See this little bird fly free.

Author Bio:

Sheila McGill started writing poetry at her Mum's bedside after her terminal cancer diagnosis. She was bereft and so, on a small Nokia E71 mobile phone, she started writing. She carried on through her Dad's terminal cancer too, and continues today with a daily vss365 Tweet. Passionate about change, she hopes her words can make a small difference somewhere along life's rocky road, to which end she is currently working on several writing projects.

GABRIELA MARIE MILTON (ED.)

216

I Am Not The Cause of Pain

by Sacha Amanda Manik

Something sits so deep within, I can't escape the feeling
that it's my fault that he's in pain, that I obstruct his healing
that I am the cause of all his sadness, anger, pain and
stress
if only I could be more love, more perfect, he would find
rest

It is like deep within 'my little child' has this 'mental stain'
convinced that it is her fault her parents are in pain
convinced that if she just were better her mother wouldn't
leave
her father wouldn't be depressed, and he would not re-
trieve

The trauma of abandonment has created this illusion of
the mind
a story of imperfections and rejections that I seem unable
to rewind
unable to untangle me from my own and his illusions
I feed the beast of separateness with narratives of confu-
sions

But when I feel deep within, not trying to escape the
feeling
the confusion vanishes and reveals an opportunity for
healing
to see that it's not my imperfections that are the root cause
to other beings' vibrational pain of losing contact with 'the
source'

Scars

by Sacha Amanda Manik

Scars on my body I've been afraid to share
if you would reject me, I couldn't bear
I try all I can to heal the unloved and damaged
but the scars of my life let my freedom be banished

Scars on my soul I've been afraid to share
if you would in truth turn out not to care
I try to heal the distorted, the needy vanity
but the scars of my life throw me into insanity

Scars in my heart I've been afraid to share
if you of my loneliness became aware
I try so hard to heal the void in my heart
by loving my scars, to love them as art

Thanking the scars for playing their part
in showing me where I from love am apart
for their unspoken ability to tell me the truth
"We, your scars, are your story but not truly you"

Author Bio:

Sacha's poetry is about her inner journey from loss, sadness and separation towards healing internal wounds and the experience of 'coming back home' to the light in her heart. Her poetry focuses mainly on the challenges of relationships and their opportunities for transforming life into an ever more profound realization of divine love and light. Find Sacha's poetry blog at https://heartlight.blog/ or on IG @heartlightpoetry

Who Determines

by Monique

Who determines
what it means to live
a life that matters
who will consider
what women go through
to be where they are today
we sat on our stories
of being overlooked
being accepted on other terms
than we'd choose for ourselves
sometimes the finger presses
on a painful pattern
scattering stereotypes
my knapsack of memories
what it's like being a woman
half a century to go on
there's still much to come
the world will change with us
or we'll bend the sky above

Author Bio:

True introvert Monique started writing in 2018 and has produced poems daily since. She has been published in several anthologies and enjoys interaction through her poetry, which enables her to communicate her feelings to the outside world. You can find her on Twitter: @starfish_72

Spark of Madness

by Dee Min

She's brave
this friend of mine
wrestling with her mind
riding the emotional swings of low to high
looking up from below sadness, fighting through to light
she writes, open and vulnerable
she writes through the lows
she dances, free and courageous
she dances through the highs
freedom to just be
they think she's mad
See
it's they who are uncomfortable with joy
See
it's she who's open to just be wherever she be
See
she embraces spark of madness
See
she drifts off to sleep, awakens, she does it again
See
this brave friend of mine
See
she knows more of what it means to be—FREE

Author Bio:

Dee Min is a poet, speaker, and author. She is an unapologetic lover of God and nature. Her work has been published in various anthologies, magazines and newspapers. Her first book is entitled *Moments: A Poetic Heart Journey*. She works for an international organization to promote social progress, better living standards and human rights.

Marriage
by Virginia Mateias

Wonder came first at your eyes, so deep and green,
at your singing, by my side,
at your tenderness, when night comes!
A caress came second, like a gust of wind...
not the touch of human hand
but a tide that lingered on my trembling, weeping skin!
"Oh, if only it weren't for your skin, that thing to separate
us,"
you'd whisper in my mind
"This obstacle is killing me!
Allow me by your side, one with your flesh to be, and if you
would let me be your guide,
there's no darkness, you will see!"
Amazed and weakened, as I fell asleep
these words a murmur to the deep:
"From now on, I won't need my skin, no more"
and saying this I grabbed it and I tore
one being we shall be forevermore! ...
I don't recall my memories, myself
only at full moon, I walk sometimes.
Two deep, green eyes watching me, out of the dirty pond,
giggling at me, double-tongued!

Unborn
by Virginia Mateias

There were 24 hours
when he picked my soul
lying beside the pearly shells.
His strong body sank into my depth,
branded it like a master his slave.
I don't need it and it's worthless for you
he said disgusted by my well-rounded womb.
If only I'd had a whole soul and the summer sun in my
mind.
If only I'd dared to be myself and hadn't been stalled by
words!

There was a basement, in a hellish hospital
a dire doctor with an ordinary blade
on a bed of pain I danced with death a final tango.

Sometimes, during moonlit nights,
dull laments intertwine.
It's the choir of babies looking for their mothers
it's the cry of women marred by their scar.

Author Bio:

Virginia Mateias is an internationally published author. Her literary work has appeared in various magazines and anthologies. She has published three volumes of poetry: *Persistence of Memory*, Sfinx 2000 publishing house, *In the shadow of the angel*, 2019, ASLRQ publishing house and *Words of Fire* [co-authored with Gabriela Marie Milton] 2022 Amanda Edit publishing house. This year she completed the children's novel *GreenlandOs* which promotes ecological and moral values.

GABRIELA MARIE MILTON (ED.)

A Woman as She Laments

by Michelle Ayon Navajas

you have called me by all sorts of names
names, my mind could not understand and process,
derogatory and degrading.
how did I become a whore when I carry children of our own
for nine months
struggling as I survive?
how did I become useless when that alone
proved more of my worth and my significance?

you have called me by all sorts of names
names, my heart could not recognize,
humiliating and demeaning.
how did I become ignorant when I took on running our
household for years alone?
how did I become stupid when that alone verified more of
my intellectual ability and common sense?

you have called me by all sorts of names
names, my soul could not fathom,
disparaging and belittling.
how did I become imbecile when I made you the great man
that you are?
how did I become moron when that alone is a testament
of my good sense and sound judgment in all practicalities?

I lament as you murdered my integrity
I lament as you slaughtered my dignity
I lament as you butchered my self-esteem
I lament as you killed my pride

you can assassinate me however you want
but you can never topple down my spirit

Angel

by Michelle Ayon Navajas

I mourn for the loss of a smile I would never be amused
I grieve for a morning cry I would never hear and ask why
I weep for the for the non-stop cuddle I would never try

then I pause and wonder

would she stare at me as I talk?
would she get quiet when I sing?
would she be intrigued when I make funny voices?
would she prefer poetry reading over singing?

I shed tears over a million times for the angelic voice I
would never hear
I weep for the baby steps I may never get to witness
I agonize for the children's party I would never get to cele-
brate

then I pause and ponder

it's time to fold and keep with ache in my heart, everything
that I have
everything that I gathered to welcome her in this world
everything that I collected to safeguard her supposed
joyful birth

then I pause and pray for our little angel in heaven

231

Author Bio:

Michelle has authored five books: *After – Rain Skies: A Million Stars* for Perak Women for Women Society (PWW), Ipoh, Perak Malaysia during their One Million Stars To End Violence campaign, *What If Snowflakes Don't Fall In Winter, Oh, Dear One!, I Would Fly To Where You Are*, and her Amazon best-selling poetry book *I Will Love You Forever, Too*. A former college professor, she is a published author at Spillwords NYC and other international literary magazines and journals.

A Single Drop

by Steph Ondrusek

I did it again:
The pain was sharp—a twinge, a gasp, a swear. I didn't
think I had done it again, but I did.
I looked at it and saw the blood seep out slowly at first,
forming its bubble, pooling, drawing, knitting together
and then pop! It gushed out, rushing over the sides of the
container created by its own design. It tried to stay together, it really did; I can almost hear it apologizing, because
it's a part of me, my very essence; more than just fluid runs
through my veins.
I watched it for a second like I always do.
My head began to get light and I turned on the faucet. The
water doesn't get cold here in the summer. A lack of insula-
tion, less fluff than would be ideal. A theme.
It stings.
I headed to the bathroom to wrap it in gauze, knowing I'd
have to change it and rip the wound open again. Oh well,
the bleeding needs to stop.
I return to the counter to meet a sharp edge again, this
time the pointer finger.
Less deep, less shocking, still brilliant red.
"Why did you do that?" comes through a text message.
"Because I don't learn from physical pain," a loaded reply. I
wonder if he notices. Probably not.
I pool and I knit and I gather.

I'm trying not to spill over the edges, but
here
we
go.

∞

by Steph Ondrusek

Time ticks by at a rate all its own—minutes crawl then move in dollops, collapsing into themselves in the process of ballooning outward towards the ether. I wonder if we could do the same: can we move despite the constraints we've placed upon ourselves? Outside the meaning we've made in an environment dedicated to our destruction? I don't know, but I know we can try.

I remember constantly aching to grow up. When I'm 8, I thought as I trudged up the hill, that's when it'll all turn a corner. 8 sounds like a cool number, like a big kid, a kid who knows what she's doing. Why 8, you ask, and I'll direct you to my younger self: she already answered.

I wish I could remember the first time I doubted myself. The moment I stopped trusting myself. Did I ever? I must have: look at the confidence in that thought, the conviction that an end to the pain I didn't know how to name would round those smooth curves of the number 8 to come to my rescue. Or, I would move along those s-bends and come to my own.

It's been 25 years since then, and I'm finally learning how.

Author Bio:

Steph Ondrusek has been disappearing into stories for a lifetime. She reads, writes, and watches fantasy, horror, science fiction, and thrillers—best when combined. Steph is a student of human dynamics: having worked a decade as a health coach and recently transitioned to liberation work and consulting, her curiosity has led her to devote her life to the examination of power and people.

She Came Off The Edge of The Cliff

by Asha Ozra

She came off the edge of the cliff,
and not a soul to hold her hand,
but her resolve never faltered,
she has learnt to heal her wounds,
never the need to justify herself,
now she proudly carried,
that child under her heart,
a nameless child that no one wanted,
an invisible angel who has kissed,
all her scars,
and was now her *raison d'être*.

She Was A Flower

by Asha Ozra

She was a flower who grew up in the dirt,
the nestling that fell out of its nest,
but still feathered her broken wings,
she was the orphan child who looked up,
at the bright stars in dark nights,
making promises for a better life,
how many years did she cry in the dark,
to wear a beautiful smile during daylight?
Every morning putting her pride aside,
slowly building up her strength,
until the day she became the heroine,
of her own story.

Author Bio:

Asha describes herself as 'An ordinary girl with an ordinary life.' Her name, meaning 'hope' was also her grandmother's. She shares her late grandmother's passion for books and words, and enjoys writing poetry.

Brick
by Ali Olsen

red brick reason
black and white thinking
obsidian reflections
ink splash introspection
letters of desperation
an undiagnosed infection
had me swimming in insanity
hijacked my personality
for fifteen years I was—
not me.
it's all in your head
the doctor's said and labeled
a hysterical woman
the oldest tale I fought,
antibiotics healed me
forgiveness saved me
and gratitude gave me
peace for what I
survived,
I survived.

Loom
by Ali Olsen

the loom holds
the thorns and seeds
the scars it stitched,
the generational trauma
in my family tree

the veins in my
leaf, no longer read
woe is me—
even when I weep
I water the seeds

the weave stopped
the bleeding and here I am
laced up tight,
not a victim,
just proud I survived

Author Bio:

Ali Olsen is a Poet, Lyme Warrior, Mother of a Child with Autism and Married to a Veteran, LGBTQIA (she/her).

Path of Defiance
by A. L. O'Prunty

An independent nature, that was me,
head in the clouds, that was me too

They wanted to fit me in their mold
fine-tune my brain as the weaker sex-
incapable of clear thought

The battles were many,
open wounds seeped through my future:
was I on the road to self-awareness
or the road named, Disaster?

A need for approval grew within
self-image was seen through eyes of others
they had broken me, and my spirit
till that independent little girl remembered her worth...

Slamming the door on the face of failure
the vortex of violence endured
walking through the fear, I changed my future
enriching the lives of others

Author Bio:

A. L. O'Prunty, also known as Poetess O'Prunty, has been writing poetry since her first hand-bound chapbook at the age of ten. Her poems have been published in newspapers, anthologies, e-zines and on several online literary sites. To her credit, Middle Island Press has published her poetry books, *Selected Snippets* and *Unfolding Hearts*. O'Prunty is the mother of three adult children and has three grand-children. She calls the rolling hills of Wild, Wonderful West Virginia, home.

Too Much of You

by Renata Pavrey

Too tall, they said; you tower above us all
too short and stumpy, you're hidden in a crowd
too thin, you'll blow away in a breeze
too fat, Oh! You must love food
put on some weight, lose some weight
no one will look at you; but they always look
you reveal too much skin
you're boring, dressed from head to toe
your shorts are too short, your skirts are too long
your shirts are too loose, your pants are too tight
you're too soft and timid; too loud and outspoken
you won't get far without enough money
too much money will get to your head
too slow, too fast
too strong, too weak
too much, too little
that's what everyone says
they ask everyone, but you
listen to everyone, but you
you don't count because you're too you
double yourself up and become two of too
because you're just too much of you
don't let them stop you.

Author Bio:

Renata Pavrey is a widely published writer and poet. Her poems, essays, reviews, artwork and stories have been featured in journals, magazines, zines, books and podcasts. Renata is a nutritionist and Pilates teacher, an Odissi dancer, marathon runner and linguaphile. She reads across genres and languages, and her writing follows suit. She can be reached @writerlylegacy on Twitter.

Prêt-à-Porter
by Basiliké Pappa

too big / too small / too long / too short / too high / too low
No dress can ever fit you – wrong bird for the right trap /
wrong princess for the right frog / wrong hand for the right
job. Even your feet are far too big and no shoe can ever fit.

too bright / too dark / too soft / too sharp / too standard /
too avant-garde

These tongues grow thick by swallowing their own saliva.
A house is no jail, they say, but you know a house has more
walls than windows. And if you are a plant, you are all
roots, no leaves. If you are a book, you are covered in dust.
If you are a candle, you have to be burned to be of use. If
you are a thing, you must be an invisible, silent thing. And
if you have a soul, they say, it's just a pinprick.

too old / too young / too good / too bad / too simple / too
complex

Make a world of you. Take a tour through your every sense,
sink your teeth in everything. And if you are a book, write
yourself. If you are a thing, fall off the shelf like hell. Candle? – no: you're a star: stay as you are. If you are a tree,
make a thousand leaves. Learn how to make your own
dresses: it's an act of faith. If you are a flower, don't be
afraid to blossom. If you are a bud, you are made of

dreams anyway. If you are a song, be everything you feel.

If you are a wind, blow where you want. If you are a river, flow, and if you are a bird, fly. If you are a tooth, bite. Tell no lies. Be strong, soft, generous: make a game of it. And never care what a stranger thinks when you take hold of the universe and shake it, or make the wild sea the mirror of your face.

Rebellion Swerve
by Basiliké Pappa

I flex the fingers. My fingers.
These are my arms. I have three freckles on my right shoul-
der.
These are my eyes. Brown. They are mine.
This is me.

I tie a hundred suns around my hips. I cherry-paint my lips,
kohl-draw my eye lines.

The drums are earth, the ney is wind and I am cymbals,
shimmies, the tiniest shivers, motes of dust caught in a ray
of light, hip swerves, skirt swirls.

I shake off gaze tropes / sacred assumptions / polar standards / demands / ignorant myths / madonna-whoring /
disclaimers / advice / unsolicited appetites / rules / labels /
anger (fear) / judgment / expectations / projections / stereotypes: out of my way / out of sight / out of mind.
And so they turn to stone –flat sun-washed stone– for my
bare feet to dance on.

Author Bio:

Basiliké Pappa lives in Greece. Her work has appeared in *Ubu.*, *Carmina Magazine*, *Heron Tree*, *Punk Noir*, *Sledgehammer Lit*, *Glitchwords*, *11 Mag Berlin*, *Rat's Ass Review*, *Dodging the Rain*, *Eunoia Review*, *Surreal Poetics*, *Bones Journal for Contemporary Haiku*, *Sonic Boom*, *Visual Verse*, *Timeless Tales* and *Intrinsick*.

Performance

by Vasiliki Petroudi

She's frozen, petrified,
her eyes looking at the headlights like a terrified deer
she clenches her fists
her nails hurt the skin, she welcomes the pain,
pain's good now, will give her strength
crowd is waiting, all eyes on her, silence
she looks at the corner of the stage, her little angel is smiling at her,
his lips whisper "you can do it mommy"
she turns to the keyboarder "give me a beat"
and the words flow like a stream, microphone is on fire,
she's fierce now, her rhymes catch people's hearts
listen world, listen to my poems, let me tell you about pain,
about the nights I spent on the kitchen floor beaten and
bruised,
let me tell you about the nights I was hiding my face with
shame
because I was raped once more in my own house
let me tell you about my journey, my breakthrough to
freedom
let me tell you about your story
yours
and yours and yours...

Suits

by Vasiliki Petroudi

It is in the late hours when she finally allows herself to let
it go
between the headache and sore muscles
those low torturing voices pounding her relentlessly,
questioning every decision, raking up every single moment,
pointing out the mistakes
tentacles of anxiety clench more during the night
when the rush of the day lessens
under her fancy suit and makeup just a tired woman
who longs for something to hold on
no one is waiting for her at home
her identity is lost through corridors and offices
last drawer on the left,
under the case files a picture of a girl on the beach
she is holding it close to her heart, a lonely tear, a sigh
she's not that girl anymore and there's no time for the
beach
she knows she can't go back
so the only thing left for her is to move forward

Author Bio:

Vasiliki Petroudi is a 45-year-old married mother of two. She
left her job as a graphic designer and history of art teacher
to follow her dream of becoming an author.

A Warrior Rose
by Cynthia Padilla

Darling, you're different… you're a warrior rose growing in
a garden of gratitude,
radiating resilience the color of dusted amethyst haze. Your
courageous compassion
works its magic in everything you touch – a spell of warm
honey filling the lull of a
silent wind. But listen to the echoes from the sky reminding you: "You are enough!"

The Way of Woman
by Cynthia Padilla

The way of woman can be found in the softest inhale of a
sun-kissed hope; barefoot
she hypnotically dances like a swallow lost beneath a pink
moon; spinning her gold
glory on sacred ground, planting seeds of life's wonder –
never wasting love because
her mind only sees beauty around her: she is an enduring
enigma.

Author Bio:

Cynthia Padilla is a lawyer and content designer from Los Angeles, California. She enjoys writing poetry as a creative outlet for her busy life. Cynthia has been published in several anthologies and maintains a poetry account on Instagram: @cynthiapadillajd_poetry. A lover of music, she is also an avid vinyl record collector.

Labels
by Punam

The labels you anoint me with
tell your story more than mine
dark, skinny, curly-haired, woman
you think you are calling me just names!
You colour shame me, you body shame me
you also gender shame me.
you brand my soul with your disparaging tone
I fit none of the parameters
that you superciliously set for me

Existing on the periphery of existence
I become the nobody you want me to be
writhing in shame and guilt
blaming my birth for my miserable life
if only I could wither to invisibility
the mortification of being, a burden too heavy!

My shrivelled soul retires reticently
cowering cowardly from the ignominy
I dip my fingers in the tears you force me to shed
and scribble
for letting my fingers speak
is like bloodletting
it eases my pain and soothes my heart

Bit by bit liquid emotions seep out
crystallising on a white, pristine sheet
the shame, the poison, the worthlessness
all drain out syllable after syllable
but the shining words that appear
on the unsullied paper
are of belief, self-worth and determination

Now what is left is just me
me, as I am,
not me, as you want
and this is the me I should be.

Healing
by Punam

I sit with Band-Aid, dressing and gauze
wondering from where to start
it is useless to ponder about the cause
even though I am left with a broken heart

Wondering from where to start
I decide to ignore the jagged edges
even though I am left with a broken heart
I can avoid falling off the ledges

I decide to ignore the jagged edges
to begin the process to mend
I can avoid falling off the ledges
I must not be rigid but bend

To begin the process to mend
dwelling on the past will not help
I must not be rigid but bend
painful memories I should skelp

Dwelling on the past will not help
love is the only regular salve to be used
painful memories I should skelp
nobody in this world is un-bruised

Love is the only regular salve to be used
it is useless to ponder about the cause
nobody in this world is un-bruised
I sit with Band-Aid, dressing and gauze

Author Bio:

Punam is a sailor's wife and stay at home mom of two teen-
agers. Words and rhymes fascinated her since school time.
She has been blogging at paeansunpluggedblog.wordpress.
com since 2016. Some of her poems have found a home in
Spillwords Publications, *Visual Verse*, *Tuck Magazine* and *Indian Periodical.*

Your Girl...
by Pamela Pfautsch

We can tell ourselves we are badass women, that boss
lady, grandmother, mother, auntie,
sister, wife, and girlfriend.

One who slaved, hurt, and loved for what we needed to
accomplish.

No apologies for being that girl who had to work, scratch,
and claw to stand with you.

Wanting to be free, didn't want to be held down, but with
you together forever.

Have your back with mad respect to birth your dreams,
and carry your hopes in my hands.

You are finding me when I am lost to hold my hand in endless love.

Didn't miss the lessons to teach me how to love you right,
asking you to read through the
pages of my book to learn about me.

The girl that I was raised to be.

Author Bio:

Pamela is an educator and former journalist living in Frisco, Texas. She has submitted poems to Robert Lee Brewer's blog: *Poetic Asides* since 2016

Boudica's Soliloquy

by Dawn Pisturino

Foul deeds of war have broken me.
Come, smell the blood! Hear the moans of the dying!
The corpses of my daughters lay silently at my feet,
shamed and murdered by our Roman tormentors.
Colchester and London – what glorious victories! –
The blood flowed freely from Roman wounds.
They howled in rage as they died. How we cheered!
But Rome's crawling legions caught us in their snare,
and now, we are vanquished.
Britannia is no more. Weep for a chastised people!
No longer Queen, I am marked for death.
No longer Mother, I will not be consoled.
No longer Wife, I burn with revenge.
I lift the flask of poison to my lips, tasting the bitterness in
my mouth.
I will lie here with my daughters, my shield across my
breast
and my spear by my side, and welcome Death with honor.

Author Bio:

Dawn Pisturino is a licensed registered nurse in Arizona whose publishing credits include poems, limericks, short stories, and articles.

Behind My Façade
by RajaShree

You judge me from my smile; and
have no idea of my pain; that
struggles to hide at the threshold of my eyes
and at the collage of my lips,
as I suppress the outburst
and try to shine a little brighter.
My heart has built a huge fort around itself;
my pain also doesn't get consent
to liberate from its shackle;
tell me how can I feel love?

So, I end up creating a façade
with my fairy-tale smile;
and like a lush greenery,
it hides my grief of decades…
wanting to find a release.
 ~ Strong Woman

Resilience Is My Name
by RajaShree

Just like a kite,
flying against the winds,
I emerge through the tempest of my life;
and am finding my way back to myself.
Born to soar high;
no turbulence can define my fate.
I rose then,
will rise again;
Resilience is my name.

Author Bio:

Rajashree (a.k.a. Defiant Sunflower) is an Indian poet and Copywriter living in Kolkata, the City of Joy. She writes about love, life, hope inspiration, and rebellion. She aims to write experiences, to make you feel that you are not alone; we all have our heartbreaks, we all can heal. You can find her on Instagram: @defiantsunflower

Bird of Promise
by Nancy Richy

It was just a fling, just one of those things she fell upon
quite by accident with no intent of malice or harm.
She never meant for the strong desire so wrong to last this
long.
No child, she. A life well spent with no sense or scent of
doubt or regret
for she was a one-off, a rare and spirited bird of promise in
thought, action and word.
She knew herself better than any woman or man who
came to her with open heart and hand,
never afraid to take a stand, without trying she could
command
a room of strangers or friends for she was the willow that
always bends.
Never intimidated, she wouldn't allow herself to be
berated, deflated, abused or humiliated.
Then this thing, this once in a lifetime fling blossomed like
the bouquets of spring,
bursting with an uncontrollable, unstoppable, insurmount-
able force she could not rein in.
How did she allow herself to be so exposed, for him to see
her inner core,
wanting and demanding more than she could give or
afford
while inflicting pain with nothing to gain except stress and
blame

GABRIELA MARIE MILTON (ED.)

and risking the loss of all things she held near and dear,
almost extinguishing her brightest inner flame.
Resolve restored she said, "No more!" She'd said it before,
two, three times, maybe four.
Get up off the floor, open the door; be that bird of promise
and soar.
This time she meant it but her heart was broken and sore
like those who suffered and bore
the ravages of war.

The Shells

by Nancy Richy

Shells scattered along the shore
some glittering in the golden sunlight
lapis lazuli kisses of blue and green upon the water
so wondrous in their radiant beauty
delicate as the blossoms of a dewy lilac tree
day and night the waves wash over the shells
yet they retain their brilliant resilience
trodden upon by eyes bewitched by shooting stars
in the blackness of the night
some are picked up and tossed into the sea
only to return upon the next wave
those trampled into the sand do not sink
they are not swallowed up nor do they disappear
for as fragile and tenuous as they may appear
they stand the eternal test of time
ever rising as an Easter Morn
for they are the She Shells
they are women

Author Bio:

Nancy is a first-generation Sicilian, wife, mom, Grammy, friend, writer, musician, singer, dreamer and lover of all things Beatles. She has recently achieved her dream of becoming a published author. She belongs to several writing groups and has narrated a number of her pieces on "Upload", a popular BBC Radio program. She has a website on WordPress where she posts further examples of her work.

The Sounds I Hear
by Carol Roberts

The sounds I hear
the only way I will ever know you
psychosis or twin-flame love
up to the ink burning my soul
when I walk
the fear shadowed land
telepathically close
the rhythm of your heart
we are but frequencies
pulses of time
yesterday's failings
forging tomorrow's hand
the mirrored sun
the ache of wanting
ashes and memories
bringing you ever closer
into the tender shadow's weep
I will lay my spirit
I will tell the story
the way I hear it
you will lay
the matching pieces
there is rage in love
there is love in rage

Dawn's Mystical
by Carol Roberts

Dawn's mystical,
misty call
starburst dreams
fading into a haze
what the light didn't catch
what remains buried
whispers,
velvet to the touch
we strive to know
turning over our hearts
savour the loss
feel the pain
why are we so dark
what is the attraction
the shadowed ones
acrylic in the hue
we hold on
to haunted memories
to the gossamer shroud
of who we are
and when we finally
understand the melody
we can absolve
all that was
and will ever be

Author Bio:

Carol Roberts is an author and member of the Visionary Fiction Alliance. She writes visionary/metaphysical genre cross fantasy. She is also a freelance writer with particular interest in cultural myth. Originally from Vienna, she has spent all of her adult life in New Zealand. Her work took her to several different countries, where she indulged her fascination with stories. Her publisher Clean Reads has released her novels *Atlantis* and *Tower of Babel*.

.

Secure

by Grace Y. Estevez-Reddy

Sorry that my hair is curly, sorry my body is curvy,
so sorry your eyes must see, every last bit that makes me,
me.

So sorry that I'm not enough, or that I act a little rough.
So sorry you can't understand, or accept me, the way I am.

So sorry that I felt this way, so happy that my views have
swayed.
Never sorry for who I am, instead grateful, I took a stand.

So happy that my hair has waves, so happy I am now so
brave,
enough to laugh off all critique, loving myself, being
unique.

So happy that I never broke, so happy I no longer choke,
I know that I was made perfect, not put on earth as an
object.

So grateful for all that I know, so grateful I now run my
show.
Teaching others, what life taught me, not dictating who
they should be.

Control

by Grace Y. Estevez-Reddy

Your weapon of choice, a piercing harsh tongue, the most hurtful shots fly straight through her lungs, leaving her breathless, shaken to her core, dismiss all emotions, by slamming their doors.

Your ego is so strong it eats at her soul, she tries to hold on, but gives up control, her mind is all bruised, along with her heart, too strong to let go, too weak to depart.

Alone in the cold, nowhere else to be, no money for food, afraid of the streets. Fearful to go home, she already left, slowly walking back, with stones in her chest. She looks for an option, searching hard for strength, finds answers inside, while holding her breath. The slowest exhale releases her pain, you may hold her body, but never her brain.

Embracing the moment, the time is right now, she knows she will make it, but does not know how. Decides not to enter, instead turns around, will start from the bottom, pull up from the ground. The sun shines so bright, glistens on her face, she may be unstable, but will find her place. Good riddance to you, she has no regrets, knowing she is ready to pass any test.

Author Bio:

Grace Y. Estevez-Reddy has always had a passion for poetry. While students were paying attention to their teachers, Grace was staring outside the window and writing poetry to describe her emotions. A natural empath with an appreciation for the meaning behind everything, she enjoys imagining what it would be like to walk in the shoes of others. Grace lives in the beautiful mountains of Western North Carolina with her husband, children, and two dogs.

GABRIELA MARIE MILTON (ED.)

A Single Mother's Work
by Kim M. Russell

Always the last one to arrive,
drop your child off, say goodbye
and run to catch the bus,
but you got by.

The school has just been on the phone,
left a message with a certain tone
that you forgot her lunch.
You weren't the only one.

Leaving work on time's a fight,
bags of shopping snagged your tights,
always last to pick her up.
Another late night.

Tucked up safely in her bed,
fair curls falling round her head,
just one more story, Mum,
and you always read.

Picking up her clothes and toys,
ears pricked for the slightest noise,
washing-up waited in the sink -
and an empty bed.

Grandmother's Shoes
by Kim M. Russell

She had a cupboard full of shoes
she couldn't throw away,
reminders of the comfy days
when every shoe would fit.

For me, it was a treasure trove
of giant shoes for a four-year-old
in which to slide across the floor,
Ginger to Granddad's Astaire.

I was completely unaware
of the agony of her size three feet,
the bunions that distorted canvas and leather
with each step in every kind of weather.

I tap-danced past the kitchen, pointing toes,
balancing on kitten heels and stilettos,
while she spread her feet in slippers,
slashed at the bulges with her pinking scissors.

Author Bio:

Kim M. Russell blogs at writinginnorthnorfolk.com; her poems have been published on-line by *Visual Verse*, Spillwords, *The Ekphrastic Review*, *Pure Haiku* and *Poetry Pea*, and in printed anthologies: *Anthology of Aunts* and *Second Place Rosette* (The Emma Press), *Peeking Cat, Fieldwork* (New Nature Writing from East Anglia) and the *Poetry Pea Journals*. She lives in Norfolk with her husband and two cats.

Strands

by Kathryn Sadakierski

You cut hair through the day, sweep the broken pieces
away,
strands and strands of time and growth pruned like
branches,
snipped and shorn, made better and brighter than they
were before.
Illumined with new life, I can see it shine,
the dead weight of what held me down,
split ends, the fractured, frayed ways of my thinking
always leading to the same self-doubt, now gone,
the shorter length of the locks framing my face
helping me to notice what I couldn't before
when I looked critically at my unsure countenance,
afraid to gaze at these features staring back at me in the
mirror.
Being hurt by others made me see myself differently,
look inside, sometimes, uncertainly,
wondering what I could ever achieve,
but you help us to lift our spirits, coaxing out the beauty
within.
Conversation, music, flows around the chair,
brooms sweeping up more tresses,
hair of every texture and color painting the canvas.
I feel like I'm visiting with friends, not at the hair cuttery,
telling you about my aspirations to teach,
letting the spark in my heart radiate when I talk about my

writing,
but it's you who helps to teach us
to love ourselves, and see what good
we have inside, all while making us look more
resplendent on the outside, because we can look with
clearer sight.
We're encouraged to face this fresh afternoon with a confident step,
to meet the day with a glowing face I can gaze back at with
hope.
It's not easy, broken backs, broken strands,
but the smiles that break across can be gifts of their own.
In every breaking, there is transformation,
and even in the scars obscuring my vision of my heart,
I came to view the sadness and pain
as being essential to my growth, the pruning and polishing
that makes me shine brighter now.
It's through people like you
that my self-doubts could be dust-panned away.
I'm led bravely forward, not lost in the past,
all because you sealed the mirror's cracks,
so when I looked in the glass, I saw I wasn't alone.
There was always another who had my back,
showing me the value in who I am,
and in the circle of support,
the family and friends, community I have, strands,
enduring, resilient, empowering,
forever closely woven.

Every Drop of Ink
by Kathryn Sadakierski

The words of false assumption, passing judgment on you,
fall harsh and metal-cold on the ears,
like the tin shackle around the top of a mason jar's neck,
it rings around your mind, the memory of a stereotype's
lash
searing through the hopes you'd built
for someone to be different, not the kind
who'd box you into society's rigid expectations
like everyone else,
an error like trying to name colors on a canvas
without ever looking at the painting,
never noticing the stories that unwind,
spinning on the axis of creativity and light,
uncontained by an easel's frame.

You are worth the time, rare as a shooting star
that one could only hope to see in the endless sky.
No decade, no age before
has ever met the likes of you,
since you were destined for this,
to, right now, make a difference.
You were meant to be understood, listened to,
not brushed off, like a speck of paint,
as something that you're not.
You're not only essential to the art,
but the masterpiece itself;

never are you simply crumbs
to be walked on, ignored, forgotten,
because you are whole.

I will use every ounce of my being,
every drop of ink, every line on my page,
to remind you that you are loved,
important, special, and here
where you're meant to flourish
with the sun you have shining inside,
nurturing your dreams.
Let them grow tall
for you to see the fruit of belief,
the love that will set you free.
It starts with you, investing every ounce of being,
every drop of ink, every line on the page
to loving your endless soul,
the star tapestry, the glittering mosaic
that is you, a soul meant to be known,
treasured as life's breath itself.

Author Bio:

Kathryn Sadakierski is a 22-year-old writer whose work has appeared in *Critical Read*, *Halfway Down the Stairs*, *Literature Today*, and elsewhere. Her micro-chapbook *Travels through New York* was published by Origami Poems Project (2020). She holds a B.A. and M.S. from Bay Path University.

Gelid
by Libbie

No one knows the instinct
of their furtive colossus
as the gelid wind rushes
uncovering the invisible means
wiping the aura clean
for only then
the course of fate finds its space
and the sculpted message
suddenly swings without warning
in the sweet breeze
of a long-sought embrace
only here and now
do the souls
betide in a tranquil
and primitive caliber

Love Rising Skies
by Libbie

A mackerel sky breathing
before first light
and the gleam washes the heavens
of the many questions found
when deciphering the muddle
from the calm
as time is a wonderfully crafted moment
in the land of sentient elements

Author Bio:

Libbie, a.k.a. SoulScratches, is a female living in Austin,
Texas. Being a curious survivor, she is an advocate, nature
lover, art fan, chocolate and tea freak, and history junkie.
Scratching words and taking photographs feeds her thirst
for creativity, and helps define a wisdom gained on this
journey. She enjoys exploring environmental stewardship,
storytelling and interconnections with nature.

Please Listen
by Shammi Para

I have listened to
you long enough
now time for you
to listen to
me

I am a woman
you have come
from me

Please listen.

What are you looking
at, for
I have it all
a mind too
voluptuous in its
creativity

Will you can you
understand
once and for all
I'm more than what
your eyes see

my legs my nose
my eyes my skin
my hair

look again
and you will see

tired of birthing you
she is birthing me

labor was long
and hard
but worth it
cradling
she

to nurture to grow
to bloom
to establish
her place
in the
annals of infinity.

Sing It Loud
by Shammi Para

I was never weak
though never strong
enough to lift
bags off the ground

what kind of strength
are you looking for?

I was never weak
though never strong
I announced this
early to the world
of men and women
all around

it wasn't easy
but I knew as even
now I do and
always will
that I am I
as you are you

so stop
don't kowtow
remember this only
strength is not a monopoly

my your her
strength has always
been will be
in sinews
unseen

you and he
are not one
above the other
you and he
are equal music
side by side
together

with tectonic power
sing your song
sing it loud
free the tied verses
to the unbound

expectations
limitations
set by others
fall to the ground
dare not dare not keep
you caged and bound.

Author Bio:

Shammi Para is a published author and writer. She has written for Huffington Post US on the blogger platform, and is a contributor to Times of India's 'Speaking Tree' column.

I Paint Myself From Scratch

by Bojana Stojcic

Here, my husband's hands hold a palette and paint brush-es, casting shadows over a speck of dust in frame. He's tal-ented and strong, saintly even for bearing with me though my womb is lifeless. Me, I am gratitude for salvation, a black crosshatch pattern, shadowing and shading. The more lines I do, the darker the shading becomes. He kills cockroaches by stepping on them, hands patting his swollen belly, jokes how my Muse likes to take long, unscheduled breaks, swears I'm the one he'd die in a ditch for. All the while I stand still against the wall like a twisted tree trunk, hide behind his words and muse on silence. Obviously, I never knew how to draw the line. Obviously, he never knew how not to cross it. He sketches me quickly, without much preparation or con-sideration for details, although he prides himself on know-ing everything about me, down to the last detail, and I ... I tried on the role of wife to see how it fit. Didn't. Doesn't. Suddenly I remembered I was born screaming, sticking my tongue out and gulping cold air into my lungs. I took all my charms and threw them in the recycle bin, thought they might make pencils out of them someday. And when I told him I want to die naked, bruised and bleeding, hands hold-ing all the dead children I birthed, he puffed out his fleshy cheeks letting out a lungful of steamy breath. "They'll de-spise you for stripping away your skin," he said. Made me thank the good Lord for staying alive, shed the bloodied rags away from my body and move on. He'll paint me no more. Here, I paint my own story with a heavy heart and hot smoke in my mouth, questioning why he brings me pain.

Author Bio:

Bojana Stojcic is an art lover, a teacher, a writer, a poet, a mom, a woman pressing on against all odds. Because the question is not who's going to let me, but rather who's going to stop me. Until she finds beautiful homes for her flash and microfiction/prose poetry collections, she'll keep submitting her work to various literary journals and magazines. She has been published in *Rust + Moth, Anti-Heroin Chic, X-R-A-Y, Mojave Heart Review, Porridge Magazine, The Blue Nib*, Spillwords, *Versification*, and elsewhere. She lives in Germany.

A Hero for My Time

by Merril D. Smith

In every war throughout all time,
women are called to reap and sow
to sew and cook, to make more from less—
to work as hard as any man, but in a dress.

In the second war to end all wars
my tiny mother bucked rivets with a larger Rosie
while ignorant men proffered vicious slurs, benighted,
as women from all backgrounds stood united.

She wanted to paint, draw, design—
but it was marriage and family—till that corroded and
exploded—
when she retired, art transpired.
(Her first show in her eighties.)

She was there—always—when I needed her,
and my siblings and I were there when she needed us—

after all, we learned from the best, or so to me, it seems—
a tiny woman who bucked rivets, painted flowers, and gave
us dreams.

A Vindication

by Merril D. Smith

To the men who saw me as a pretty toy,
the professor who joked "You don't look that smart,"
the other in grad school who tried to seduce me—
you made me doubt my worth.
But surface-beauty is ephemeral,
within me, I hold the infinite,
time has forged stellar fire and iron into steel—
I hold the strength of generations, sing the songs of stars.

Author Bio:

Merril D. Smith is a historian and poet who lives in southern New Jersey. She is the author of several books on gender and history. Her poetry has appeared in *Black Bough Poetry, Anti-Heroin Chic,* and *Fevers of the Mind*, among others. Her full-length poetry collection, *River Ghosts*, was recently published by Nightingale and Sparrow Press.

After Party

by Tracy Shawn

My father, his booming I-am-the-man-of-the-room laugh
my mother, her eyes glowing with hope.
Of course.
Yes, of course
his face hardens after the last guest flutters away.
Compares her to the women with leonine gazes and
modern-cut waists
women, he announces with authoritarian calm, that are so
much more provocative—
so much more everything than her.
My mother does not respond,
but my eleven-year-old self does.
I march into the kitchen, plaster peanut butter on bread,
smack my lips in rebellion.
"Why don't you leave?"
I yell into the undertow of their marriage,
a life-preserver for my own future.

Creators

by Tracy Shawn

We are creators
betrayed by modern-day worship.
Grasping for our celestial mothers,
their names opaque and intangible
as November's wilting twilight.
Yet, still, we tuck secret messages
in our muse-rustled words.
Intrepid scribes,
we navigate these muscular empires
toward green-wombed forests.

Author Bio:

Tracy Shawn lives and writes on the Central Coast of California. Her most recent novel, *Floating Underwater*, is about a woman who learns how to accept her own power; her debut novel, *The Grace of Crows*, is about a woman who learns how to overcome debilitating anxiety. Shawn's short stories have appeared in *Literary Brushstrokes, Psychology Tomorrow Magazine*, and *Steel House Review* Literary Journal. She's written numerous articles for print and online publications and is currently working on her third novel.

My Power Mantra

by Amita Sanghavi

Once in a while, comes my way,
an unkind comment,
on my parenting style, or my attitude,
on my posture, or my figure,
on my colour, or my over weight,
a taunt,
meant to hurt,
and haunt.
I overcome
all negative energy,
in thought, word or deed,
that may come my way.
I choose to let it go,
decide who's worthy
to stay in my inner circle,
I just choose company
that's not toxic,
but loving and humble.
No one can take my self belief away,
no one can take my confidence away,
no one can take my peace away,
no one can take my power away,
don't mistake my silence, my grace,
for fear or timidity,
when needed,

I roar my truth, my story,
and reclaim my glory.

Author Bio:

Amita Sanghavi holds degrees in English literature and education. She is the World Poetry Canada Ambassador to Oman, and Representative to Oman as pronounced by The Art Movement, 'Images & Poesia' Italy. She teaches English at Sultan Qaboos University, Muscat.

The Effort

by Josephine Shevchenko

heels, like tipping points
trajectory...always forwards
hems short and her hips
skirted in tight brackets;
those nylon ladders
I only briefly climbed;

blouse, so softly collared
in collapsing V
exposing skin, white,
not yet from baby's milk.
Take away coffee,
folder, phone, cigarette
and slipping clutch of papers
perhaps held by the friction
of one button

a flapping
irksome breeze
she's hunchbacked
with the effort of
keeping it all
together

Poppy in Space
by Josephine Shevchenko

you can't imagine, she said, the grace of a poppy in space

and he asked, can you?

I rode one last night, we horsed among the stars
and I held its petaled mane
we galloped in the wake of a tinkered light...

it was a foaming fricassee you know, like the sun
mottled on a wave's bent knee?
and the poppy sang of love and flying
and the way the wind unites blood and skin
for cheeks like wine stains
and we soared around the bullioned headlands of galaxies.

Was this a dream? he wanted to know

Look at that sea eagle, poised like fantasy
on invisible air towers.
Do you wonder if she is a dream?
All I want you to see
is the freedom and the glory
and the tiny red dot that is me
finding my own suns.

Author Bio:

J. Shevchenko lives in Canberra, Australia and has always enjoyed writing. Despite doing a creative writing degree at university, she has lacked confidence to publish. Her blog (https://outofthecave.blog) has given her a space in which to build up her confidence. She is now in her 40s, has recently finished treatment for breast cancer, and is eager to grab life more assertively by the horns.

Our Bodies Are Welcome Mats
by Cherie Lynae Cabrera Suski

From her first step
the yolk or femininity weighed her down
shoulders built for invisible loads
painting it pink doesn't make it weigh less
her distilled values grind her down
into monetary and aesthetic uses
surrounded by cat calls and pop quizzes
will she ever be good enough?

What if peace feels like poetry
tiny explosions in our chests
the release of emotions from their tidy schedules
minds wondering and translating
fingers itching for a pen?

Why does safety feel like prose
the fiction of escapism
fades away when we close our book
and grip our pepper spray to our chest
are our bodies welcoming mats?

When did my name become a song
the lyrics a dirge
of the mundane and absurd
our syllables stretched by baritones?

Pearls and Gold
by Cherie Lynae Cabrera Suski

I can't pronounce my name correctly
my tongue refuses the trill of pride
tripping on whether I belong
on both sides

my ancestors crossed bodies of water
to make this place their home
oceans and rivers bore witness

I'm a blurb in a pile of poems
I'm an island
a place where colors blend
and cultures are watered down

my people can't recognize me
and refuse my existence
though I'm labeled exotic
a human, but distant

my parent's love was once illegal
secret kisses bloomed into a secret marriage
which birthed confused children
my mother's hands in my father's
like pearls and gold
like passion and rebellion
a mixture that forever glows

Author Bio:

Cherie Lynae Cabrera Suski is a Labor and Delivery nurse from Washington state. She recently published her short story, *The Betrothal Trials*, with Dragon Soul Press, and her poem, *Why We Love*, with Fifth Wheel Press. Her bachelor's degree in anthropology from the University of Washington focused on Race, Class, and Gender and her experience as a neurodivergent Chicana helps her represent diversity in her writing. She is currently querying her debut novel, *I Am Armageddon*.

Torn From Home

by Michele Lee Sefton

Smaller and smaller our house became.
We turned a corner, and it was gone.
My room, my school, my friends – gone.
Would I ever see them again?
No conversation, no explanation.
Riding in the back of our truck, with the luggage
      tossed over bumps
      hair tangled by hot air
      dry eyes did sting
      leather tongue tasting bugs
      covered in sadness, sweat, and dust
Miles and miles
with no escape from the wind or heat,
wondering what would become of us, of me.
My mom and stepdad inside the cool cab.
My brother and I whipped outside.
Hold on, pray, hide.
Tighter and tighter
my youthful spirit was squeezed.
Somewhere across the vast lands of Texas it left me
a broken girl ripped from her home, torn from her world.
Just before starry skies gave way to a hazy sunrise,
I saw it flickering above the hard flatbed –
a neon sign that flashed, "Mote_"
Home sweet home for the next six weeks.
Long days spent alone in a pink-painted abode

near the Corpus Christi Bay where we trapped crabs
when the workday was done. Legs torn
from boiled bodies that squealed and fought to live.
No escape. Melted butter did not sweeten the pain.

Finding Home
by Michele Lee Sefton

A vision born when I was a young girl,
living in a Texas motel, lulled me to sleep,
and gave me hope. Thousands of times I have travelled
a road that leads to a home I have never touched
but know quite well.

Sprawling grass painted pristine green,
a spacious porch for lazy afternoons,
and sturdy pillars that support and impress
replaced the home, from which I was torn.
Eyes closed, I see myself walking up the steps,
toward a door that protects
my secret dreams.

I don't need to knock; I simply turn the key.
My life and all I hoped it to be, found inside,
sheltered by an antique vintage façade.

This vision saved me from drowning
when I was a young girl, barely surviving.
A life imagined has carried me
through the darkest of days.
Returning again and again
to that guarded sanctuary.

The vision that pulls me forward,
has remained out of reach.
With this truth, I am at peace.
Four decades later, I finally see:
the home with the strong foundation, is me.

Author Bio:

Michele Lee Sefton is a veteran high school English teacher, writer, poet, and blogger at MyInspiredLife.org. She is the published author of three illustrated poetry collections: *Being a Woman – Overcoming, Being a Woman – Becoming, and Being a Woman – Forthcoming*. Her forth publication, *My Inspired Life – A Poetic Journey*, celebrates a blogging milestone and includes her photography. Her first novel, a coming-of-age story written in poetic prose, is in the editorial stage of publication. Her writing has also been published by the National Association for Poetry Therapy (*The Muse-letter*); Piper Center for Creative Writing at Arizona State University (*Piper Poetry Month Anthology*) and elsewhere. She assists the author of 'The Story You Need to Tell,' Sandra Marinella, with weekly narrative therapy workshops. When she isn't writing or co-facilitating online, she enjoys photography and dancing, as a NIA practitioner and teacher (mind-body fusion fitness).

Tapestry of Life
by Christine Seery

A heavy textile she wears gracefully
like a second skin it clings,
both suffocating and liberating her
with grief and hopeful possibilities.

Distress and melancholy
come together artfully
in magnificent plum and brown,
tightly woven with a twist.

Radiant on her wedding day,
intertwining an ethereal white
with plum and brown
faithfully braided with love.

Mourning grandma's death,
a tragic onyx cloud
follows the ethereal white
sewn with sorrowful tears.

New life arrives,
baby doll pink now reigns
dulling the pain of the onyx cloud.
Stitched in pure joy.

A devastating miscarriage,
baby doll pink melts away
to a painful deep indigo loss.
Fastened together with sorrow.

Her tapestry is a wonder,
twice as long as it used to be,
and will grow forevermore.
Beautiful and dark,
light and hopeful
just like her.

I Call Her Grandma
by Christine Seery

A lifetime of hardship
strapped to her back
her young daughter gone too soon
leaving a weeping woman
who just kept going
her essence soothing
an angel disguised as an old lady
complete with talcum powder hugs
silkily delicate skin
more strength than a hundred men
single mother to three
she was gifted with endless patience
that the weight of the world
rested so gracefully on her shoulders
her smile, brilliantly full of life
even in the harshest of weather
she glowed like a glittering star
shining down, guiding my heart home
I call her grandma

Author Bio:

Christine Seery is a 38-year-old stay at home mom. Christine uses her struggles with mental health as inspiration for her writing. She has had work published in Down In The Dirt magazine, The Stray Branch, Bewildering Stories, Piker Press, and Wolff Poetry Literary Journal. She lives in Ohio with her husband and daughter. Her hobbies are journaling, reading, and collecting skulls and masquerade masks.

After The Deployment

by Tricia Sankey

She was excited to pick him up at the airport.
It was snowing that day, and she realized right
then, how soft sky can sting.
It'd been one year since he was deployed to the desert
and she was cold the whole time. Now, like a snow-covered branch,
her anxiety weighed heavy. She feared she would snap and
graze power lines.
The crowds shook her. Would he see she was different?
Would there be changes in him?
Sometimes strength is admitting it's been hard.
Deep breath.

Armywife
by Tricia Sankey

She floats above the chaos
    a tired three-year old in the backseat and a
    yappy Yorkie on her lap. One thousand miles
    to go – desert this time – Fort Huachuca
    is a word she must learn to say right.

He knows she'll blossom in the rocks
    for she's cracked hard spots with
    each move. She just raises her
    chin and leans
        into bright sun.

Author Bio:

Tricia Sankey is an armywife who enjoys blogging her poetry and flash fiction at www.triciasankey.com. You can follow her on Twitter @triciasankey. Her novella, *The Light in the Cave*, is available on Amazon.

Within Me

by Shailja Sharma

Picking up my broken pieces
putting them together
to realize:
I was the problem and
I was my own clue
pats on my back and
steps walking by my step
yet my weight was carried by own two feet
treading through forests unknown
chasing the fragrance of the flower that
my mind had grown
pricked by thorns
dodged by petals that
I could not touch or see
following the dew drops in
search of the bud
to realize:
it was all *within me*
I was the broken piece and
I was my own glue

Agni: The Fire
by Shailja Sharma

She was profound
she was pure
she was deep
her eyes were intense and her perspective had an impact
like the pleats of the sky
she meant what she said and did what she meant
she cared like a flame warming the cold face of Earth
hugging the whole humanity
she walked the sun like it was her baby
sprinkling stars from her sparking eyes
killing the ignorant darkness
like a powerful flame
her power is love
she is who she is
her love is deep and it is pure
she is profound
she is *The Fire*

Author Bio:

Shailja Sharma (Ph.D.), USA, is a mental health provider and a multilingual author. Apart from scholarly publication and editorial service, her literary writings have been nationally and internationally published. She is currently serving on the editing panel of a UK-based journal of poetry and artwork related to themes of mental health, health, illness, the mind, the brain, and the body. Dr. Sharma's publications have appeared in many literary journals/forums including *Beautiful Space*, Spillwords, *Literary Heist*, Piker Press, *Better Than Starbucks, Life in 10*, Masticadores, and *Setu*. She is the author of a poetry book, *Dear Mama: An Immigrant's Secret Cry*, by Pittsburgh-based Setu. Her next collection, *Sip the Roses* is upcoming via ABP Press, USA.

GABRIELA MARIE MILTON (ED.)

320

Resolution

by Audrey Semprun

Boundaries call - beckon - intrude
stifling who I am, imposing upon me laws - demands -
offenses
but who am I to stop - to yield - to submit
have I not lived transgressions like a soiled garment a
taboo - a shame
loosen me from these chains that bind
that trespass like so many hands against my innocence -
against my weathered brow
leave me to my own defense to my own sense of being
leave me to be my own judge and jury and if I transgress
know that I have weighed myself and I find myself wanting,
but even still, I am able to make sound judgement without
molestation.
A liberated woman of sound mind and soul.
Now, I more than plead.
I demand that you remove these chains from me and leave
me be - free.

Murder on My Mind

by Audrey Semprun

Go ahead, go to bed
go ahead, sleep
I'm going to burn you - you just watch me
and then he came at me savagely
the beast - the man
the man I had married
but that was then, that young dreamer only wanting him
and for him to hold me
coming at me with rage and murder in his eyes
funny, I don't even know why I had provoked him so
all that I do know is that it wasn't the only time I had murder on my mind
I got out after much pain and much sorrow, so fortunate to
have another tomorrow
finally, I ran, I ran away from him - away from his rage, his
anger, his sin
and I never looked back - never looked back again
the children and I journeyed, and we suffered great lack,
but we were strong, we refused to look back - Oh, for a
hope and a future

Author Bio:

Audrey Semprun lives a quiet life with her husband, Al. The couple has been married for over 30 years. Audrey's past experience with domestic violence, and then as a single parent of three small children taught her how to not only survive, but to thrive in a world that wasn't always fair, nor always kind. Audrey works as a Publisher of her own Neighborhood magazine.

GABRIELA MARIE MILTON (ED.)

In Time and Torn Memories
by Dawn Serbert

In time and torn memories,
every page of me reads
differently...

For I hold the fall of where I came undone,

But I also neighbour the clock
that turned on me,
that told me I could never be~

Yet here I am,

A butterfly ascending...
the sins of my invoice
their embroidered shame now...

for I always remembered
my scars were stars,
I always knew my autism...

Was my kingdom...

      My home

I Am Me
by Dawn Serbert

Flutter me wayward
I am written beautifully now,
a water droplet of the girl
I used to be…
Jupiter over moondust
I conquered the expectations
of oblivion's plough,
and…
I am stronger than the kiss
they try to breathe,
I am wiser than the vines
they tried to bleed,
I am imperfect,
I am enough,

     I am me...

Author Bio:

Dawn Serbert is a poet who realises that she is so much more than other people's definition of her: she describes this as 'her superpower.'

In The Heather
by Sal

Tired of the status quo
I run
till my lungs
can take no more
and when
laughter and lament
merge into one thought
I sow my words
in the heather
and I am finally heard

Me

by Sal

in the ledgers of life
your pristine page entries
they mock me
we threw promises in the fire
in stark detail
they hound me
under the canopy of
the weeping willows
I buried my tears in the ground
I'm so much more than you see
in the quiet moments
I am the most me

Author Bio:

Sal works as a Business Analyst in the IT sector. Her written pieces are essentially journals; a way to balance out the monotony of the corporate world. Seeing people connect with her writing brings her boundless joy.

Forgiveness
by Enola Ton

From a savage childhood
to a broken womanhood
the wounds I have healed
are wounds I have honored
and the scars you don't see
are the most hard won
in those hidden places
where lethal damage was done
requiring the salve of forgiveness
a crucial ointment
to be applied again and again
because wounds of shattered dignity
can be concealed, but not untraced
and wounds irrigated in forgiveness
can be healed,
but not erased.

Wounded Worth (A Reverse Etheree Poem)
by Enola Ton

as worth, words, and tears healed my deepest shame
I learned to walk away from false blame
when I witnessed my own gall spew
frayed bitterness flew
I let myself be seen
clothed in dignity
royal remnants
woven from
wounded
worth

Author Bio:

Enola Ton is a survivor and overcomer of chronic childhood abuse and trauma. For most of her adult life she has worked with at-risk youth alongside her husband at a youth ranch in AR. They have three grown children and eight grandchildren and now live on the east coast of Florida. She has written one poetry book under her pen name, Enola Ton, in the form of letters between her younger and older self. Available on Amazon. You can find her on Twitter @enolatonlori. She is working on a second poetry book that will focus on living victoriously while living with damage. Her heart's desire is for survivors to know they are not alone.

Back Then

by Fizzy

Back then walking under a shadow
everything was them and all else
the shadow was lifted
finally no them no else
years later walking further and further
the shadow dissipated
the new way had been made
a new horizon in play
freedom swaying like a constant breeze

Author Bio:

Fizzy Twizler is 48 years old and hails from London. Part of the Dark Poet Society of Twitter (Quill and Crow Publications) with various micro fiction and poems published in anthologies on Amazon, and online magazines.

GABRIELA MARIE MILTON (ED.)

·

Dark Night's End
by C.X. Turner

despair weighs heavy on my skin tonight
greedy in the silence

along the tired spine of stillness
a single candle drifts

ever-flickering flame
beyond the secrets we keep

tousle of a gentle stranger, sighs surrender in the fog
permeating all

my edges, I kneel at the shoreline
fingers feeling for the thirst

velvet to the touch
I taste blossom of morning, soft dew on my lips

crawl all the way through to find me
without you

within a sleeping silver dawn --
still gleaming, deeply full

Light in The Dark
by C.X. Turner

I undress my wounds
wear them with pride
tuck scribbled notes of self-love
in my purse, reminders
someone loves me

On days when the deep ache
of self-loathing bites hard
I pull at shards of broken scars
midnight morphine
warmly wrapped shame

Take the notes out!
Let the rain fall dark
I have enough light in me
to see the world differently
be who I know I am -- free

Author Bio:

C.X.Turner (she/her) is a poet and registered social care professional living in the UK. She loves the brevity of Japanese
haiku and senryū short-form poetry. Recently published in
Kingfisher, MasticadoresUsa, *cattails, Wales Haiku, Failed
Haiku, Prune Juice, Cold Moon* & more. Find her on Twitter
@lover__poetic.

One Strong Megan
by M. Taggart

I almost lost Megan.
Last Tuesday Megan stayed home from work.
Just before noon I heard my name called from upstairs.
Followed by the sound of Megan landing on the bathroom floor.
I was downstairs feeding Gavin his lunch.

Megan's head was in between the toilet and the shower.
She was just opening her eyes.
Her breathing was highly elevated. She was perspiring heavily.
I started asking basic questions. She wasn't able to focus her eyes.
From my point of view, Megan did not know who I was.

I flat lined emotionally. Everything slowed down.
I had my cell phone in my hand while asking Megan,
"Would you like an ambulance?"
I was calling regardless of her answer. She was pregnant.
We found out the previous Friday night that the pregnancy was ectopic.
Monday morning she had a follow up with her doctor to confirm
what the emergency room told her Friday night.
Her doctor gave her two shots of metho, told her she might feel cramping,

but that she'd be able to go to work on Tuesday.

There I squatted, on Tuesday, brushing the hair from Megan's face.
"Yes, she's starting to come to. Yes, she knows who she is. No, her color seems alright. (I am color blind.)
Honey, they are telling me to tell you that help is on the way.
Ma'am, I need to run downstairs and get my son out of his high chair. He'll tip it over.
Yes, I'll be fast and I'll come back up to be with Megan."

Thank God Megan is strong.

The doctor was wrong. The worst possible situation was happening.
Megan had suffered a rupture and was bleeding internally.

"Be a good boy, Gavin." I had just placed Gavin in his nursery area.
I ran back upstairs.

"Ma'am I can hear the sirens, I'm going to let you go."

"Megan, you're going to be O.K. The ambulance is outside. I'll be right back. I need to open the door for them."

"Yes, please come in. She's directly up the stairs and straight into the bathroom."

"Gavin, Mommy is going to be OK. Please don't cry. Please don't cry."

I called Megan's sister while the ambulance drove away. "Get to the Hospital. Call me as soon as you know if she'll need surgery."

Megan was rushed into emergency surgery.
She was bleeding so badly they were literally watching her stomach rise.
Her blood pressure was becoming close to even. I arrived at the hospital too late.
I stood in line to be told where she was. Her sister appeared and told me they couldn't wait any longer. They didn't know I was standing in line at the front desk. No cell reception.

The surgeon, Lillian, saved Megan's life. Lillian was, and is amazing.
"Mr. Taggart, she suffered internal damage. The pregnancy ruptured.
She lost 1.3 liters of blood. She bled into her abdomen. There was other damage too.
Would you like to see the pictures? We had no choice. We believe we did the right thing."

"Megan was close to death. We didn't have time."
Megan was literally dying on our bathroom floor. Somehow she made it to surgery.

Her pregnancy hormones were 31k at her doctor's office.
We were told the cut off for the medicine administered to
my wife is 5k.

Directly after Megan's surgery Megan fainted in the bathroom.
Two nurses held her in place until a team of nurses helped
to carry
her back to her bed. I stood watching. Arms folded. Useless. Straight faced.
Upset, for what my wife was being forced to endure. Megan
was anemic
and now needed a blood transfusion. After her surgery we
were told they
tried to remove all of the blood that had bled into her
abdomen,
but that it was impossible to do. The remaining blood
would slowly be absorbed.
However, the process would be painful. Blood is an irritant
when placed where
it ought not be. Megan struggled to move for a number
days.

Family arrived from numerous states to help. Help support
us.
To help watch Gavin so I could sleep next to Megan at the
hospital.
This event surrendered us, placed us in a position of hope
and sadness.

It affected our entire family structure and friends. Megan is
so very loved by so many.

Now though, as we near Christmas, we are thankful.
We are trying to focus on the positive. Megan will be home
with us.
She can read to Gavin. She can sit with Gavin and play with
dinosaurs.
She can tell him she loves him and give him kisses.
But please Gavin, no jumping on Mommy.
Let's just be happy that you have your mother.
The thought of Gavin growing up without Megan is too
devastating for me to process.

Megan is finally home and resting.
She has a long recovery in front of her.
She won't be returning to work until after Christmas.
She can't lift over ten pounds for six weeks.
She can't lift our son. She can't rock our son.
This has stolen a portion of her life.
Megan has been afraid to sleep for fear of not waking up.
When she does sleep she has nightmares.

The night we brought Megan home,
I said to myself 'My head closed today.'
It was Megan's strength that opened my mind again.
Megan wanted the most simple thing in life after having
nearly lost hers, love. She wanted love.
So, we'll drive after the sun goes down

and enjoy showing Gavin the Christmas lights.
We'll drive on the dirt roads and look for Dinos in the forest.
We'll watch Christmas movies.
We'll place Gavin next to Mommy
and let the cuddles begin. It's time to build memories.

I said I almost lost my wife. Megan was too strong to let that happen.

Author Bio:

M. Taggart is a loving father and husband. His work was published in America's Emerging Literary Fiction Writers: Northeast Regions, 2019 (Z Publishing House), America's Emerging Horror Writers: East Region, 2019 (Z Publishing House), Massachusetts's Emerging Writers; An Anthology of Fiction, 2018 (Z Publishing House), Vita Brevis Press, *The Drabble, Literary Yard, Proletaria, MasticadoresUsa, MasticadoresIndia*. His short story "Bodies in the Basement" was nominated and elected publication of the year (non-poetic) Spillwords Press, 2019. He blogs at https://mtaggartwriter.wordpress.com/.

The Tangible Trauma

by Parvatha Varthini

An Abstract picture in the mirror,
she watched herself with eyes clear.
When too little creatures grew hastily,
life's destruction began massively.
To rise with brightness like a Sun,
she had to sacrifice like a nun.
Phases of human life she knew,
but the stages of struggles are new.
Busy in counting the twinkling stars,
she forgot to nurture the Moon on par.
As solving this puzzle demanded a price,
she could give nothing but her slice.
Emotional dramas she never enjoyed,
hence decided to keep her overjoyed.
She believes, the purpose is served,
to enchant,
to enliven.

The Scarlet Secret
by Parvatha Varthini

A Fortunate day!!!
Exclaimed elders spotting it.
Stains, she knew not could change her life.
Now, the balancing act is required
in this cycle, not with pedals but with rebels.
Once in two fortnight,
she visits without an invite.
Though only a sojourn each time,
the aches and agony it gives
is a never-ending journey.
Still, she endures it with ease,
as it would halt one fortunate day,
to crown her with the best reward.
She gets ready for a combat inside her
between a queen and million invaders.
More like a svayamvara it is
where she chooses the strongest.
Worship her, for she has healed wounds
not just for one kingdom but for the world…

Author Bio:

Parvatha Varthini, is a doctoral student doing research on Post Humanism. She resides in Chennai and she has degrees in English Literature from MK University. Her passion for teaching has enabled her to pursue online tutoring.

Excommunicate
by Vanessa V

Excommunicate
the word is stuck in my brain
a sheer headache

I don't complain
I even hug the vicious thorns
a searing pain

I fool by my laughs
a mere sad echo
of hollow insides

I waltz through this life
my head held high
with deep chaos inside

The mask I wear
a facade to conceal
this storm always brewing inside

Excommunicate
the word I self-imposed
for soiled I was

It Wasn't The Right Key

by Vanessa V

It wasn't the right key playing
behind perfectly closed door

My life he has been singing
out of tune

My pain he has been strumming
with his fingers

My soul he has been killing
with hurtful words

My universe he has been smashing
for nothingness

He always leaves me painted in blue
in silence

My soul is screaming
to be set free
for worthy I am
of love, of sunlight

The fragility of your soul
will demean me no more
The petals of my soul
will always stand strong

Author Bio:

Vanessa is new to creative writing, which she finds to be a good tool for healing. She uses her poetry to bring awareness of domestic abuse and violence.

GABRIELA MARIE MILTON (ED.)

She Rose

by Margareth Waterboer

From deep within the dungeon of despair she rose!
FREE from his terrifying and threatening stranglehold
free from red rivulets that from wounds and tender flesh
flowed
free from humiliation and purple welts, stark reminders of
a death expected and felt
from her meagre battery of artillery she collected mettle
and grit - then rose
fearlessly she looked down upon the wretched scourge,
dangling from the rafters of inferiority
as his pathetic pleas echoed from the walls of her impervi-
ous apathy
her laughter drowned the comedy - her winged soul was
finally flying into the heart of liberty

Audacious and resolute on the lonely and ambitious path
she reached her sovereign state -
her esteemed personal domain upon the immovable rock
of edification
in victorious hands she finally brandished the strongest
weapon of them all -
a Bachelor's degree - reward for fortitude in a fierce battle
for independence
an undeniable sceptre of authority and symbol of triumph
over male dominance

from the soul-weary core of a once battered female phy-
sique, a tenacious goddess rose-
a Marianne who broke the challenging chains of her private
unbearable domestic Bastille
where insecurity paraded as masculine legitimate authority …BUT she broke fee …and ROSE!

Beautiful Bruised Butterflies

by Margareth Waterboer

His lovely little protégé, he said, the only blooming flower
of his heart
stealing stolen kisses and planting secret notes with hearts
and butterflies
sharing covert nods to reaffirm clandestine tryst with furtive glances and smiles
and in all naivety she let his teaching hands and reassuring
whispers
mould her to her trusted loving master's perfect artistry
but busy bees buzzed around her ears, whispering of other
crushed butterflies
whimpering in dark lonely rooms, trampled under his
wandering feet
from crippling shock she rose with steady wings – ready to
fly into war territory
she'd be their voice of redemption – flapping fierce venge-
ance around his calm confidence
on her high pedestal she climbed, surrounded by all
bruised butterflies
undaunted by repercussions she addressed the thief of
their precious innocence
man of immorality, she said, philanderer and unrivalled
liar
here is your entire concubine whose trust you crushed–
never again shall you be the spear of our misery

or corruptor of the innocent and vulnerable
today we surrender female frailty and take back our power
your secret will resound in a court of law, for truth and
justice -
and away they fluttered from the red-faced, shivering pup-
pet master
confident of their own rebirth in Life's cleansing and healing garden

Author Bio:

Margareth Waterboer is a retired South African English lec-
turer, married mother of two adult children and two grand-
sons. Despite her sparkling personality, her poetry leans
towards the melancholic – with themes of rejection and
disloyalty, injustice, desolation and misery. She takes inspiration for her poetry from the quiet and peaceful environment of nature.

Cyclical Rebirth
by Ingrid Wilson

Every month I die, and am reborn
with dark-day demons, whispering me home:
this is no cause to cry, or be forlorn

Another night of anguish, pages torn
from out the book of life, a weighty tome
for every month I die, and am reborn

As in your arms, I find my cares are borne
aloft, alight, through sky and wild sea-foam
there is no cause to cry, or be forlorn

Across my weathered face, the lines are worn
like scars upon a beach I walk alone
where every month I die, and am reborn

Distant, I hear the bright triumphal horn
sounding its rallying call, as clarion
for there's no cause to cry, or be forlorn

The dark births light, cast in poetic form
of ancient bards, who, lyre-in-hand, still roam
through centuries, to die, and be reborn:
without a cause to cry, or be forlorn

Growing Through My Pain
by Ingrid Wilson

I do believe I'm growing through my pain
though sometimes when the knife twists I still wince
I will not stoop to hate myself again.

Though sometimes when the knife twists I still wince
actions or words of others are their own
I've learned this and I've practiced ever since.

Actions and words of others are their own
as my own treasure house is my own soul
and knowing this, I face my fears alone.

As my own treasure house is my own soul
I have fought long, I have fought hard to keep it
and in self-keeping, still my dreams are whole.

I have fought long, I have fought hard to keep it
you cannot have it now, e'en if you would
it's my reward, and only I shall reap it.

So as I take my leave of you, refrain
from telling me my pain has done no good:
I do believe I'm growing through my pain
I will not stoop to hate myself again

Author Bio:

Ingrid is the owner and editor of the publishing house 'Experiments in Fiction.' She has been writing poetry since childhood, and more recently has launched her passion for writing into a career. A featured contributor at *Masticadore-sUSA*, and bartender at dVerse Poets' Pub, Ingrid has had her writing published in many online publications and print journals. She published her first solo poetry collection, *40 Poems at 40*, via EIF in February 2022. She is also a PMDD warrior, and advocates for better healthcare and education around PMDD (Pre-Menstrual Dysphoric Disorder). The poem 'Cyclical Rebirth' describes her experience of PMDD.

GABRIELA MARIE MILTON (ED.)

Into No-Man's Land

by Lisa Walker

Slow steel-eyed scythe cuts flash lines, releasing dark
clouds and Demons outwards across great green ethereal
plains where my solitary soul wanders, lost and aching.
Tears splash down my mud-cracked face, salt droplets
bouncing off parched soil along deep-fissured fault lines.
Growth stunted. Starved of nutrients, hope, light.
Under steady transition of sun and moon, barren soil, clod-
heavy, life-cycles to fertility.
Fragility and responsibility sharp-focused, pressing deep.
Breath bursts out in horrific gasps, going against grain of
Nature, blowing tumbleweed dreams
into No Man's Land.
Darwin tells us survival weeds out weakness; my life's im-
perfections must still be tended to.
My roots reach down deep to penetrate Earth's core and
pull strength determined. Stretch up

Into branches.
Into light.   Into flight.
Into freedom.

Only to come, NOW, to exist in abstract hollowness. Sturdy and beautiful bark encasing rot and ruin. Cellular core, diseased from within. Strong façade standing tall.
Still reaching for cerulean skies; patient, strong/flawed, faltering.
Leaning into wind as fierce-dark-storm gathers on horizon.

Personal Growth
by Lisa Walker

Youth's heart bloomed, fresh-full of earnest intentions.
Gifted whole and wrapped in petals of deep red rose and
purest pale cherry blossom. Tenderly, one heart became
two. Love's pulse quickened, deep-dwelling kaleidoscope
of butterflies.

In the reflective mirror, childish innocence comes back
foolish. Fidelity and home quickly squandered. Youth's
heart stabbed sharp:
Penetrating trauma. Knife, dripping. Brutal crimson stain.
Heart bleeding and torn.
Needed to run, to create shelter and a quiet place.
Years of mending (took patience, hope and survival).
Heart's neat and careful restoration diligently undertaken
and achieved. Then dust, neglect, obscurity. Heart stashed
away in the bottom drawer. Buried underneath lace table-
cloths and careful safe stitches of foremothers.

After:
A surprising sea breeze blew in through (land-locked)
open window. In the sunrise glow, my one soul met itself
(in another). Two stayed, after sunset. Love seeped into
blood, and bones. Mended heart wholly returned, firm, to
my chest. Not gifted away. Kept safe (in me, as me, is me) -
where it belongs. When love is true, we do not need to gift
our hearts away.

True hearts grow together (to-get-her) and bloom.

Author Bio:

Lisa Walker is a graduate of the University of Nottingham, with a Bachelor of Arts degree in American Studies with Canadian Studies. Lisa started writing poetry in January 2022. Her writing often draws inspiration from her experience of living with the chronic illness ME/CFS and her love of the outdoors and Nature.

The Great Escape

by Jia-Li Yang (Cassa Bassa)

She packed two silk dresses and seven different red lip-
sticks
caught the midnight train to Paris
the rhythm of train lulled her to the memory of yesterdays

She was cut off from the world that she once lived in vi-
brancy
by a pair of cruel hands clasped around her neck
deceiving her as a silk tie but deadly
light went out of her in that luxurious villa
her shadow ghost roamed among the Spanish antique
furniture and priceless artworks
she pressed her pale face on the tan sandstone wall longing for the sun to rescue her
she envied the robins sang freely in the midst of bluebells
and primroses
the night was starless
but she saw Van Gogh's *Cafe de nuit*
and smelled the roses wrapped in newspaper resting casu-
ally on the table by a *café allongé*
the soft song of *J'en connais* calling her home

Author Bio:

Jia-Li Yang (Cassa Bassa) works with disadvantaged people in Sydney, Australia. She is constantly inspired by their resilience and strength.

Her work has been published in the *Australian Poetry Journal*; *The Poets Symphony*; *Creation and the Cosmos* published by Raw Earth Ink. and *Heart Beats* published by Prolific Pulse. She blogs at: https://flickerofthoughts.com.

Made in the USA
Monee, IL
07 July 2022